Brenda-
Be sure to
make the
journey
matter!

-Elise

Brenda –
& Sur to
rake the
squirre
path

Praise for
Leading Through the Turn

"No matter where you are on your leadership journey, you'll want to read *Leading Through the Turn*. Elise's story is both inspiring and thought-provoking. She walks us step-by-step through her own evolution as a leader and the many practical lessons learned along the way. Through her remarkable experiences, she has emerged with a new perspective on leadership that breaks through the shallow definitions of the past, painting a far more compelling picture of what a satisfying leadership experience looks like."

—JOHN C. MAXWELL
New York Times bestselling author, speaker,
and Leadership Expert

"Leadership is far more than just achieving the traditional marks of success. It's about finding true significance in what we do. *Leading Through the Turn* will make you rethink your purpose and redefine your destination. Elise teaches us that the journey isn't just a means to an end; it's something to be savored and experienced. A must-read for every leader today."

—JOHN ADDISON
former Co-CEO of Primerica;
Wall Street Journal bestselling author of "Real Leadership"
and Leadership Editor, *Success Magazine*

"This is such a fresh take on leadership—an in-the-trenches handbook from a leader who has found far more than just success in her journey. Elise inspires us to live a whole life, to make a positive difference for those we love and lead, and most important, to enjoy the ride along the way. Authentic and compelling, you'll definitely want this one on your leadership bookshelf."

—DONNA WIEDERKEHR
CMO, Dentsu Aegis Network, Americas

"In her well-crafted, highly instructive new book, Elise Mitchell shares an intimate view of her professional journey, learnings, personal growth, and transformation. *Leading Through the Turn* is captivating reading for would-be entrepreneurs and leaders set on reinventing their future with new-found tools and perspective."

—DAVE POTTRUCK
former CEO, Charles Schwab;
Chairman of the Board, Hightower

LEADING
THROUGH
THE TURN

How a Journey
Mindset Can Help
Leaders Find Success
and Significance

ELISE S. MITCHELL

New York Chicago San Francisco Athens London Madrid
Mexico City Milan New Delhi Singapore Sydney Toronto

3 4 5 6 7 8 9   LCR   21 20 19 18

ISBN   978-1-259-86099-7
MHID   1-259-86099-X

e-ISBN   978-1-259-86100-0
e-MHID   1-259-86100-7

This publication is designed to provide accurate and authoritative information in regard to the subject matter covered. It is sold with the understanding that neither the author nor the publisher is engaged in rendering legal, accounting, securities trading, or other professional services. If legal advice or other expert assistance is required, the services of a competent professional person should be sought.
   —From a Declaration of Principles Jointly Adopted by a Committee of the
      American Bar Association and a Committee of Publishers and Associations

Library of Congress Cataloging-in-Publication Data

Names: Mitchell, Elise, author.
Title: Leading through the turn : how a journey mindset can help leaders find
   success and significance / Elise Mitchell.
Description: 1 Edition. | New York : McGraw-Hill Education, 2017.
Identifiers: LCCN 2016032536 (print) | LCCN 2016051076 (ebook) | ISBN
   9781259860997 (hardback) | ISBN 125986099X | ISBN 9781259861000 () |
   ISBN 1259861007
Subjects: LCSH: Leadership. | Business planning. | Success in business. | BISAC:
   BUSINESS & ECONOMICS / Leadership.
Classification: LCC HD57.7 .M578 2017 (print) | LCC HD57.7 (ebook) | DDC
   658.4/092--dc23
LC record available at https://na01.safelinks.protection.outlook.com/?url=https
   %3A%2F%2Flccn.loc.gov%2F2016032536&data=01%7C01%7Ckari.black
   %40mheducation.com%7C03d68698a9d8408539bb08d40707b602%7Cf919
   b1efc0c347358fca0928ec39d8d5%7C1&sdata=VhtTIQutsoIuBTRRtz8vI4l7
   T%2Btct6YpV7aJNyw%2Bbpg%3D&reserved=0

This book is dedicated to my husband, Raye, and our two children, Mackenzie and Jackson. Fellow journeyers of the best kind. Thank you for being with me every step of the way.

"*I feel happy to be here, and still a little sad to be here too. Sometimes it's a little better to travel than to arrive.*"

—ROBERT M. PIRSIG
Zen and the Art of Motorcycle Maintenance

Contents

PART III

Enjoying the Ride

Acknowledgments

If I've learned anything on this leadership journey, it's how to surround myself with smart people who know a lot about things I don't. Any project of significance takes an entire team to pull it off properly. This book, of course, is no different. Writing it has been an incredible experience, a powerful time of reflection and appreciation, and many people have helped me reach the destination of author. I'm thankful to all of them.

My parents, of course, from the beginning set me off on this journey, and more importantly showed me the beauty of what a leader's life grounded in integrity and guided by goodness looks like. They also patiently read the manuscript of this book in its earliest stages and gave me valuable insights and suggestions to make it better.

My husband, Raye, and our children, Mackenzie and Jackson, have inspired me, challenged me, and supported me. They've loved me for who I am, regardless of where the journey has led us. Being a wife and a mom have been the best jobs I've ever had, and I am blessed to be part of their lives.

The team at Mitchell Communications Group—those who are with us now and those who have been here through the years—I couldn't have done any of this without you. This dream team has helped shape me as a leader, as a professional, and as a friend. They have put up with me at my worst and inspired me to be my best. Special thanks to the visionaries and risk-takers who did some heavy lifting along the way to help make Mitchell what it is now, especially Michael Clark, Sarah Clark, Blake Woolsey, Marla Hunt, Heather Ellington, Larry Templeton, Kate Andersen, Holly Gilbert, Cydnee Cochran, and Jameson Sheppard. Many of them were first to the party and loyal through the years. Thanks also to my erstwhile assistant, Lori Johnson, who does far more for me than anyone should have to, not to mention keeping me on schedule.

I'm thankful for our more than 70 current clients at Mitchell and the many others over the past two decades who have allowed us to work alongside them. It's been a privilege to help them build their companies' relationships, enhance their reputations, and achieve results that have made a meaningful difference for their businesses.

To my new friends and colleagues throughout Dentsu Aegis Network worldwide who have stretched me and helped me reach heights I never imagined—I am so grateful you are part of my life today. Particularly, Tim Andree, who believed in me as a leader and valued our agency enough to buy it. Of all our suitors, Tim and Dentsu were the right match for us, and we are privileged to be part of the Dentsu Aegis global family. And to Rob Horler, who has continued to champion my vision and dream of building a world-class PR capability—I'm lucky to call you my boss and thankful for your entrepreneurial spirit.

Early on in the writing process, I corralled a few trusted advisors and friends who have been a part of this 20-year ride at Mitchell in some way and who could give me meaningful advice. When I started this process, I wanted to write about all the perfect and smart things I have done through the years, but you have them to thank for challenging me to write about all the hard stuff real leaders face every day—fear, failure, doubt, confusion, and loss. Thank goodness. Their encouragement prompted me to share the authentic story of a leader's journey and how difficult it really is, especially the path of entrepreneurship. I think this book is a far better read because of their vision. Thank you Blake Woolsey, Sarah Clark, David Roth, Stephen Caldwell, Michael Lasky, and Peggi Einhorn—all of whom have helped me refine the message I wanted to share. I am a better author for the guidance they gave me along the way. And there weren't that many perfect and smart things anyway.

Several proven business leaders contributed in a very specific way to this book by giving of their time and allowing me to interview them and share their wisdom. Thanks to Wendy Davidson, Mike Duke, Harold Korell, Kara Trott, Julia Hood, Tim Andree, Jennifer Smith, Tommy Van Zandt, Cheryl Bacon, and Kent and Amber Brantly. I could write a book on each one of them and the powerful way they are being destination leaders with a journey mindset. I am inspired by them, grateful for their impact on my leadership experience, and thankful for their friendship.

I'm indebted to Heidi Krupp (agent extraordinaire) and Darren Lisiten of Krupp Kommunications. From the first time I met her, Heidi saw what I couldn't see and pushed me to bring this book to other leaders. She lit a fire under me that few have been able to do. I aspire to have as much energy and passion for life as Heidi does. There is no one like her.

Donya Dickerson, Courtney Fischer, and the team at McGraw-Hill Education deserve special thanks. I'll never forget my first phone conversation with Donya—standing behind a vending machine at the U.S. Naval Academy on a football game weekend selling her on my idea for a leadership book that could help leaders lead at their best. She believed in this book from that first call and has supported my writing throughout the entire process. Thank you, McGraw-Hill Education, for making my idea a reality.

Finally, I'm thankful to God for giving me a relentless drive to achieve the unlikely, talents beyond what I deserve, unexpected opportunities to use them, and for calling me to give all the good stuff away—the higher calling of leadership. May I reach this destination.

The View from the Cargo Hold

Never mind that we've been planning this trip for six months. My husband and I are standing in line to board a flight from Dallas to Zurich, and I'm still struggling to unplug from my life. I lob in one last call from my cell phone to the office as the agent scans my boarding pass. I'm greeted with laughter on the other end of the line. "Go on vacation," they tell me. I suppose I should.

From the beginning, I must confess that I am a destination person, much more interested in being somewhere than experiencing the journey. I'm a leader with a determined focus to get there, wherever "there" might be. Friends have described me as an intensely passionate achiever with a motor that seldom slows down, much less stops, and it's hard for me to argue with that assessment. I've been on the go most of my life. Always searching for the next stop—but never stopping because there's always another achievement, the next "there," that keeps me going.

Sound familiar? Perhaps you have a similar destination-focus; if not, I suspect you know someone who does. So you know that although going full throttle has many advantages, it also has its challenges.

As I boarded the plane that day at the Dallas–Fort Worth airport in 2006, I was leaving behind a growing public relations company I had founded and nurtured for just over a decade. It was hard to let go, even for some much-needed vacation. Business was good, but like any young business, we still wanted to accomplish a lot more to claim success, and my to-do list was a mile long.

There is no rest for the entrepreneur. No matter where I traveled, work was always a part of my destination. As a hopeless achievement addict, that was just fine with me. Since founding the company in 1995, I'd never really been able to separate work from life and find the elusive balance between the two.

I wasn't always like that.

My love for travel began as a child, and in those more simple times, life was all about the journey. My earliest memories are of summertime cross-country drives from our home in Illinois to see my grandparents in California. My mother and father rode in the front, of course, with Dad driving our dark green station wagon and Mom at his side. My two older brothers were in the back seat. I sat cross-legged behind them all, riding in the cargo area with the suitcases and the Coleman cooler.

My role was to make sandwiches and pass out snacks, since we seldom indulged in a restaurant stop. But I loved every minute of it—playing the alphabet or license plate game with my brothers, watching the changing scenery as we moved westward, and counting down the miles to the next state line with great anticipation. I never tired of these adventures nor wished away the trip itself, no matter how uncomfortable the cargo hold was. Being on the journey was something I truly relished.

As I grew older, I fed my hunger for travel with more exotic journeys. At 15, I was a foreign exchange student in Würzburg, Germany, the reward for working two long years to raise funds for the trip while serving as president of the high school German club.

Two years later, my father and I took a two-week tour through Japan. I fell so deeply in love with that enchanting country that I returned a year later to live for a summer, earning my way by teaching English lessons in a language school.

Just after college graduation, my family reunited for a European trip that we still talk about—stories of flooded airports, lost luggage, missed planes, meeting Christians in hiding in East Berlin, sitting up late at night talking with a lonely innkeeper who missed her children in the States, enjoying local cuisine, and taking train rides through miles and miles of beautiful countryside.

When my husband Raye and I married, we planned and saved for as many trips as a young couple could possibly make on a limited budget. We looked forward to every journey and appreciated the chance to simply see interesting places and learn new things. We visited most of the Southeast and Midwest by driving from our home in Memphis. Then as our budget improved we also found ways to experience some other spectacular locations: skiing the Canadian Rockies, hiking in Kauai, deep-sea fishing in Cabo San Lucas.

Somewhere along the way, however, I stopped counting license plates and the journey lost its joy. The demands of parenting, building a career, and entrepreneurship began to take their toll. My approach to business and life became almost singularly focused on the destination. As the pressure increased and the stakes grew higher, my intensity and determination to succeed only escalated.

Several of my good friends and family members finally called me on this and encouraged me to take a long overdue vacation. "Get some time away," they said. "Spend time alone with your husband. Reconnect with him and with life. Find a little balance." So I began dreaming of going back to Europe, and that's how Raye and I ended up at the Dallas airport headed for Zurich.

The trip itself was a compromise. Raye had never been to Europe and had very little interest in going, at least in the way I had envisioned: seeing as many famous cities, museums, and monuments as possible and collecting as many passport stamps as we could cram in. Once again, a destination philosophy.

I challenged myself to find a solution.

"What if we toured Europe on a motorcycle?" I suggested.

Now I had his attention. Raye had long loved fast cars and motorcycles, so this idea appealed to him and soon the deal was sealed. I just had to muster up the courage to do something I'd never done before: get on a motorcycle.

Raye already was an experienced rider. He had owned and had ridden a number of bikes (at last count, we have two BMWs, a Kawasaki, and a throwback Ducati in the garage). I, too, loved speed and enjoyed the thrill of sitting behind the wheel of a sports car every now and then. But that was on four wheels. Riding through Europe's tallest mountains on two wheels was something altogether different.

The idea of it generated something inside me that I'd come to know well as a CEO: fear. The thought of crashing was certainly there, but more than that was the very real fear of giving up control. As we rode along the steep and curvy highways, I would be on the back of Raye's bike, holding on to him while letting go of my need to get us to the next "there."

There was also the far more hidden fear of coming to grips with what I was missing in my life. In the maddening pursuit of success, I knew I had been cheating myself and others out of the one thing we can never get back: time. I'd been stealing time from them and giving it to my company. Time with my kids, time with my husband, time with myself to pursue even the first personal interest or hobby. Every bit of spare time I had was going toward the Big Dream, and precious little of it was going toward things that were far more important. Have you experienced this as well? I wouldn't be surprised if it hits a little too close to home. Developing a nearly single-minded focus on success is a pretty common problem, unfortunately, with a fairly predictable outcome. So I suppose we shouldn't be surprised when everything—and everyone—else suffers. The fear of the price I might have to pay, or was already paying, for operating in overdrive was real. But I certainly didn't want to face it.

Facing my fears, however, had always been an integral part of my leadership style, a key reason, I believe, why I'd been able to find success in business and in life. So I began to believe this trip might give me the opportunity or perhaps even force me to begin thinking through some pretty real fears about letting go, what mattered most, and how to enjoy the journey again.

I had no idea just how life-changing the whole experience would be.

I got on the back of a motorcycle to spend some time with my husband. What I found was an out-of-body experience that gave me a new appreciation for the journey rather than just the destination. The sights, sounds, and smells of the trip rushed over me as we rode, sparking an explosion of physical, mental, spiritual, and sensual responses that were intoxicating. I was hooked, not just on rediscovering travel, but doing it on a bike.

Motorcycles suit me—sleek, fast, and challenging, they give an experience one just can't get when traveling in a car. Something about balancing your life while going 60 miles an hour helps you put your world in perspective. On the edge of dying at any moment, motorcycling forces you to focus on what's required to stay alive, pushing petty thoughts into the furthermost corners of your mind, where they belong. The thrill of the ride itself makes the journey matter just as much, if not more, than the destination.

Focusing on a destination, by the way, isn't necessarily a bad thing. You can get a heck of a lot done when you're a driven soul. As I said, going full throttle has its advantages. Everyone needs to know where they're going and have the inner drive that pushes them to get there, wherever there is.

For much of my adult life, my professional focus has been on creating an unlikely success story: a woman entrepreneur starting a public relations company from scratch in a small market virtually in the middle of nowhere, building it into a nationally competitive and quite profitable firm that won a string of business and industry awards, and that I eventually sold to an international corporation. We were very fortunate, no doubt. I suppose you could say we hit the jackpot.

In all honesty, though, I never set out to be big; I just wanted us to be the best. Naturally, in terms of expertise, but also I wanted to be the best leader. I wanted to build the finest company: one that not only made money, but also made a difference, created value for its clients, and was in it for its employees and its community. That was my destination. That was my "there," and it was well worth striving for.

I've achieved a great deal in life, reaching most of the destinations I set my sights on, and getting to just about every "there" that I ever desired. But I also came to realize that many of my destinations weren't all that satisfying if I arrived without having fully embraced the journey along the way. Typically driven leaders strive for goals such as:

- **Money:** Yes, there was always that, and although this is the primary focus of any business, at some point you do begin to wonder how much you really need, or more honestly, how much is enough.
- **Fame:** Public accolades are always nice and certainly reinforcing, but your "15 minutes of fame" really lasts only about that long. Then what?
- **Power:** Being in charge is a comfortable position for leaders. They are often driven by a need for control, but at what cost? Can you ever truly enable, equip, and empower others around you to share power and authority once you have it? Being a leader is lonely enough, but nearly soul-crushing if you can't do it with others you love and respect by your side.

These things were tangible measures of success, and I appreciated them like most leaders do. But they only partially satisfy, and they cannot be the be-all and end-all of your leadership pursuit. My destination philosophy as a leader, frankly, needed some balance. For me, the process of rediscovering that balance began on the Alps trip aboard the bike with Raye.

As I learned quickly on that trek, and as I've since experienced as a driver not just a rider, one of the biggest challenges motorcyclists face is handling turns. So one of the first things an instructor teaches new riders is the fundamental principle of "looking through the turn." As you approach a turn, you must look where you want to go rather than fixate on the potential hazards within the turn itself.

Like most of us, I have had my share of falls in the twists of work, life, love, and parenting. Turns are where you find the hazards. The goal is to keep your eyes focused on where you want to end up and have the courage to stay on the journey no matter where the road leads you.

The ideal of looking through the turn reminds me that one doesn't work well without the other: I have to focus on my destination while also embracing the journey. On my motorcycle adventures, I've been able to clear my mind and face some rather important questions and fears about my life, my business, my family relationships, my friendships, and my spirituality. I've sorted through the most common question I get when I speak to other leaders: How did you build such a successful company from scratch? The answer, for me, is found in both the journey and the destination—in looking and leading through the turn.

The lessons I've learned in more than 20 years as an entrepreneur and leader—the lessons I'll share throughout this book and with additional resources at www.elisemitchell.com—can help you find a balanced approach to your leadership that can lead to not only success in your balance sheets, but also something far more meaningful: significance in your work and in your life.

At one time, many people defined success by the things they acquired: the job titles, the size of the bank account, the vacations, the cars, the houses, and the country club memberships. More and more, however, people are seeking significance and working to build organizations that have a positive impact on their employees and the world around them. In addition, they want to live a full life while they're doing this, complete with friends, family, community, passion, and purpose that make life worth living.

That's exactly what destination leadership with a journey mindset looks like: great leaders achieve real success not just through a destination philosophy that allows them to accomplish great things. Truly satisfying and significant success for a leader comes from also enjoying the ride along the way, whether you're on the back of a motorcycle in Europe or taking in the view from the cargo hold of a green station wagon.

That's what I hope you'll gain from the stories and insights found in this book: an approach to leadership that will help you look through the turn, enjoy the journey, and reach the destinations that really matter in your life.

PART I

Jumping into Leadership

CHAPTER 1

Explore the Roads

I vividly remember the night before my first day on the job in my first true leadership role. I spent most of the evening trying to convince myself that the knot in my stomach was a result of something I ate. In reality, my nerves were getting the best of me, and all night long I was on the verge of being sick.

I was a young professional, about 30, stepping into a new organization and up to a new level of responsibility. While my drive and ambition were in high gear, I knew there were many things I didn't know about leadership and would have to learn quickly. Frankly, I didn't know if I could do it. I had sold myself well in the interviews and desperately wanted the opportunity, but none of my previous jobs had adequately prepared me for a highly visible leadership role in a rapidly growing corporation.

Such is life, right? How many times can anyone honestly say he or she is prepared for the next big challenge in his or her career, or personal life, for that matter? When my husband and I were set to bring home our first child from the hospital, we had to call a nurse to teach us how to change a diaper. Sad but true: we were highly focused professionals who never had much exposure to the fine art of diaper changing, let alone full-blown parenthood. But that didn't stop us from pursuing our desire to have children. We figured we'd take as many classes as we could and read every book available, but most of it we'd learn along the way. And when push came to shove, we could always call our parents for a crash course.

Regardless of where you are in your personal or professional life, the first thing you have to embrace if you want to lead with a destination philosophy and a journey perspective is a willingness to explore the roads—even if you feel unprepared, unqualified, and unsure. You prepare the best you can, but you have to willingly take that leap of faith and explore the adventures that await. I have read dozens of books on leadership and attended executive education at some of the world's finest academic institutions, but there is no substitute for a learner's mindset and roll-up-your-sleeves, on-the-job experience. That's where most of it has happened, at least for me.

I've learned not to let a lack of knowledge or my fear of failure hold me back from taking that next step even, and especially, if it's a big one. People can do more than they think they can if they have the fundamental knowledge, natural abilities, and learning attitude to figure it out as they go. Yet many leaders shrink from bigger opportunities because of their fears.

Has this happened to you? What kept you from taking that next step? Were you worried that everyone would find out you were a fraud? Did you see in hindsight how you were fully capable of leading at the next level but your fears made you your own worst enemy?

It's frustrating, I know, and believe me, I have had this kind of head trash, too, and not just early in my career but at several points along the way. Don't beat yourself up; instead, recognize what was holding you back and vow never to let that happen again. While you might have missed a chance to move your career forward, the good news is that it probably wasn't your last opportunity to lead on a bigger scale. So get yourself ready to take advantage of the road that lies ahead, know that leadership is a learner's game, and realize that those who are willing to be true explorers undoubtedly will make the most of life's adventures.

The night before my first day on the job was filled with the mental (and physical) battle raging within that said, "You can't do this job, because you never have before." I was scared to fail, frightened that my colleagues would figure out I wasn't smart enough or experienced enough (and I really wasn't experienced enough). In reality, that didn't matter. My boss had thoroughly vetted me, seen a lot of talent and drive in me, and knew I had a track record of accomplishments that told him, "She's the one."

As unsure as I felt inside, this was a road I knew I had to explore. So I jumped into the new opportunity as if it were the biggest thing that had happened to my career, and it was. I took over the public relations department at Embassy Suites, Inc., which was part of a rising publicly held corporation called the Promus Companies Incorporated, and experienced a good amount of success over the next several years. I moved through several different positions as the company evolved, and I launched a new marketing function for Embassy Suites, Hampton Inn, and Homewood Suites hotel brands that helped drive franchise growth for the years to come. It was one of my favorite gigs in my early career. Thank goodness I didn't listen to my fears the night before I started that journey.

What I did do, though, was trust my instincts and experience, which told me to exercise a journey perspective by learning all I could about the organization, the people, the industry, the competition, the business objectives, the strategy, the challenges, my predecessor's wins and mistakes. Then, and only then, could I work with my team to develop a plan that would impact the company for good.

I went on a listening tour, making appointments with key leaders to ask questions, gain their perspectives, and absorb anything else they would volunteer. I was especially careful to ask one particular question that I hoped would make all the difference: "What can I do for you?"

As you would expect, most of them were surprised and a bit skeptical that I didn't walk in saying, "I'm going to teach you about public relations. Why aren't you doing the right things already?" Instead I listened, learned, and sincerely wanted to help them succeed. I hoped they would believe, like I did, that we would all be more successful together if we helped each other.

Over time, they came to see my approach was inspired by a sincere spirit of reciprocity. Each one of them became a mentor or ally (or both). They were living, breathing road maps that helped me explore my new environment and move toward some important destinations. I was able to enlist their immediate help for what I needed most, which was information and lots of it, as well as support for our team's strategy and action plan. They appreciated what we did to help them and help the company succeed. I was invited to participate in leadership activities and speak at company events hosted by different departments where my predecessor had never been. All simply because I made it clear from the get-go: "I'm here to help."

After just a few months, my confidence grew. I realized that because of the professional experience I brought to the job and the information I was gathering through my listening tour, I could do a lot to help the company and champion opportunities for my team. More important, I had plenty of new friends who were willing to establish a mutually productive and supportive relationship that enabled us to make an impact. You can't get much better than that.

I learned a lot of lessons from that first true leadership role—lessons that weren't related to technical job skills. They were the qualities and attitudes that were shaping my individual leadership style and that would help me explore new roads for years to come. Here are a few worth remembering, regardless of where you are in your leadership journey, but especially if you're considering an expansion of your responsibilities:

First, Accept That Fear Is Often a Natural Part of Stepping Up

It's okay to be uncertain about your ability to succeed when what lies ahead is unknown. But recognize your anxiety for what it is, and don't give it too much credence. Certainly don't broadcast your anxieties to the world. What matters more is that you understand you have the assets you need to move forward with confidence: knowledge, expertise, skills, and natural abilities; these are things you've worked hard to acquire, and they say a lot about you. They are what you need to take on new responsibility, and as with what happened to me, they're probably why you were picked for the job.

Once I was in my new position, I realized I had a lot to offer, as well as a lot to learn, and I understood the balance between the two. Anytime you step into leadership, it's always going to be more challenging and more difficult than what you've been doing. It's not a lateral move. Don't be afraid to take on these challenges. Take comfort in the fact that you have talent and expertise, or else you wouldn't have been given the opportunity. You also have a lot of core qualities that will serve you well once you're in that role.

Second, Have a Learner's Mindset

Nobody knows everything they need when they take on new roles and responsibilities. No one expects you to, either. In fact, if you pretend that you do, you'll be sniffed out pretty quickly. It's far better to walk in with a healthy dose of humility and an open mind so you can invite teaching and accelerate the learning curve. Others will help if they see you are sincere in learning and succeeding.

Once you begin to learn, I'm certain you'll enjoy the experience, too, and appreciate the growth you see in yourself. I continued to learn immensely as I grew into my new corporate position, which was incredibly energizing. I began to see the direct connections among learning, applying, succeeding, and earning more opportunity. I knew enough to figure out what I could do in the short term, and I continued to learn fast enough to make a bigger impact over the long term as I became more knowledgeable, capable, and well connected. The secret was relying on the experience and instincts I brought to the table and complementing it with all that I was picking up as I moved forward. Being a quick learner will give you a running start. Being a lifelong learner will take you across the finish line.

Third, Establish Reciprocity

Make it clear from the beginning that you are there to help others as much as you would like help in return. This quality of leadership is so underrated and underused that you absolutely will be noticed and valued for demonstrating it consistently and sincerely. This has been the case for me. I have always determined to help others whenever I had the opportunity, and I've tried not to worry about what was in it for me. In reality, I have received tenfold in return for all I could possibly have done for others. This practice and proof have made me a believer in reciprocity, and I wouldn't lead any other way.

I appreciate Adam Grant's book *Give and Take*, which delves deeply into the subject of reciprocity. Studies have proven that those who are seen as genuinely interested in being a giver are far more successful than those who merely take from others, or even those who bargain for an even trade in return. Not surprisingly, leaders who are willing to be "otherish" as opposed to selfish in their pursuits have greater satisfaction in their work. They clearly see the impact of their giving efforts on others, and best of all, they are happier, according to Grant.

Another excellent read on this subject is *Influence without Authority* by Allan Cohen and David Bradford. It teaches that people are all more influential than they think because each person has something others value. By freely sharing things such as information, ideas, resources, and contacts, you have the foundation for a trusting relationship based on mutual benefit, not just on your own needs. You will undoubtedly benefit somewhere down the line. Reciprocity is established.

Fourth, Strive for Early Wins

Be willing to do whatever it takes to get up to speed and make a difference as quickly as you can. Early wins are key because people are forming initial impressions of you during the first few months on the job. Identify two or three things you can do to get some traction, and then build upon those.

Many years later in my career when I sold my company and had the opportunity to take on a global leadership role, a close friend and colleague recommended the book *The First 90 Days* by Michael Watkins, which lays out a series of strategies for successfully moving into a new position. I found it invaluable and a true field guide for leaders who are stepping up, because it helps you develop a game plan for early wins and setting a clear direction for future success.

The Called Leader

Most leaders fall into one of two categories: they are *called leaders* or they are *accidental leaders*. It's helpful to know which you are, but either way you have to explore the roads if you want to grow and succeed.

While I've often faced fears when taking on new leadership responsibilities, I've never really doubted that I wanted to lead. In fact, I consider myself a "called" leader—someone who naturally and intuitively sees leadership as a part of his or her makeup and destiny.

I've been a take-charge person since I was a child, always looking to rally others around some cause or event. I organized Monopoly and four square tournaments in my neighborhood, led our high school German club, and cochaired the annual singing competition at my college alma mater, just to cite a few examples.

For some of us, leadership is in our DNA. We spend much of our careers preparing for, finding, and realizing leadership opportunities. It's a passion and a calling. There are countless examples of natural born or called leaders:

- Margaret Thatcher, whose strong will and decisive demeanor earned her the nickname "The Iron Lady," rose through the political ranks to serve as prime minister of Great Britain for more than a decade. She was a political titan who positioned her nation as a powerful force to be reckoned with and a tireless warrior in the fight for what's right.
- Walt Disney is widely regarded as one of the most creative and passionate leaders in business. He devoted his life to bringing imagination to life for people worldwide through the Disney empire. His "be our guest" mentality helped him find unprecedented success as a leader.
- Nelson Mandela was South Africa's first black president, but he did not assume that role until after a life spent fighting apartheid in the streets of his home country and serving 27 years in prison. His legacy as a champion of equality and social justice earned him respect worldwide.

The Accidental Leader

The world is full of called leaders, but it's also full of accidental leaders. You know, people who never intended to lead but seemingly fell into it because circumstances demanded it. For example, they inherited a leadership position through a family business or became a leader out of necessity through entrepreneurship. Sometimes others unexpectedly step out of leadership, and the organization desperately needs the most qualified person to step in, whether he or she wants to or not.

Countless accidental leaders have changed an industry, a nation, or even a single community in some significant way:

- Crystal Lee Sutton was a textile worker in North Carolina who led the battle to establish a workers' union in the 1970s. She famously stood on a table in the middle of the factory with a handwritten, one-word sign: "UNION." Sutton's story inspired the movie *Norma Rae*.

- My mother, a retired microbiologist, taught for years at the university in my home town with a quiet dream of finding a way to interest young people in science. Together with a friend in the community who was equally passionate about the cause, they founded a regional Science Center. My mother was not a leader in the traditional sense, but she stepped into leadership to make a difference in her community.

- April Anthony started her career in accounting in the early 1990s but was drawn to buy a failing home health care business when she was only 25. Although she had intended to become a stay-at-home mom, instead she turned the company around and sold it. Then she founded two others, another home health care company and a technology business, that grew to nearly $600 million in combined revenue by 2015. Despite her multiple successes as a CEO and entrepreneur, she is the first to say that she considers herself an accidental leader who "fell into leadership."

None of these individuals sought leadership—and some even fought it. Each was given the opportunity to lead at a critical time, and each had to decide if he or she was willing to assume the role and responsibilities that came with it.

Taking Your Foot off the Brakes

Regardless of how we become leaders, finding the courage to explore the roads on that journey isn't always easy. Sometimes our own negativity holds us back from fearlessly moving forward. If we're honest, we recognize we aren't as successful as we would like to be in our current situation, so we wonder how we can take on anything new. Or we have a private but nagging fear that we just aren't cut out for leadership. Perhaps you've had one or more of these concerns. I've found that many of us shy away from a leadership challenge because we're listening to a voice inside our head that sounds like this:

- **"It's not me, it's this place."** This reveals our eagerness to get somewhere, anywhere other than where we are now. We're dying to shake off the dust of this place and move on to bigger and better things. When we get there, then we'll take on the challenge of leadership. But don't be fooled by the classic "grass is greener" mentality. We've all been guilty of feeling a bit victimized by various circumstances that have impeded our ability to lead at our best.

While some of that thinking might be justified, most of
it really isn't. Everyone struggles, and it's less about what
has happened to you and more about what you're doing in
response to your situation.

- **"It's not me, it's everyone else."** We avoid leadership
  because we can't find the right team to work with, we can't
  connect with the right organization that appreciates us,
  and no one understands us. This mindset keeps us from
  learning how to work well with others and accommodate
  their needs rather than expecting them to accommodate ours. It also hints at an unhealthy tendency to avoid
  accountability for what's not going right and identifying
  what we need to do to fix it.

- **"I've never been adequately trained or prepared for leadership."** If we're unqualified to lead, how can we expect
  to do it well? With this excuse, we focus heavily on our
  mistakes and weaknesses. Much of leadership, however, is
  learned along the way, a lot of it by trial and error. As I've
  mentioned before, a learner's mindset can make a world
  of difference in how we are perceived by others, as well as
  how quickly we can move through the learning curve.

Whether you're called to leadership or come to it acci-
dentally, you have to explore the new roads and accept the
challenges it presents if you're going to continue to grow. That
means embracing change and moving into the next role no matter how big the stretch, even, and especially, if it makes your
stomach turn all night.

Think about your current situation. Have you been holding yourself back from taking that next step? Perhaps you've

decided to pitch a tent and stay right where you are. It's not perfect, but at least it's not unknown. While that might sound appealing, I can promise you're going to be disappointed. Deciding to keep things as much the same as possible—or plateauing—is a waste of time and energy, and you're only fooling yourself. Here's why:

- **Where you are will change.** You don't know when or how, but it will and it's very possible it will no longer be so beautiful. Organizations make changes all the time—stopping/starting new products and services, merging and acquiring other organizations, finding and losing key customers, moving offices, even closing their doors. Change is inevitable, and even more so in the rapidly evolving business climate we live and work in today.

- **Everyone around you will change.** This is particularly true of your peers. They move on with their journey and develop as leaders. Because you've become comfortable and haven't pushed yourself to grow, you're no longer as qualified for new opportunities as they are. If you decide to leave your situation, you're not nearly as competitive for the better leadership positions. You've been left behind, in some ways a little, in other ways a lot.

- **You will change.** Growing and developing as a person is a natural process. In leadership, it's essential. You must be committed to getting better every day, even though you won't. But if you're committed, you'll keep trying and the results will come over time. There will be plenty of dips along the way, but your general trajectory must be up.

Let's face it: you can't stay where you are, because where you are won't stay the same, and neither will you, really. Change happens whether you like it or not. Instead of resisting it, use that same energy to embrace change, face uncertainty, and continue moving forward because of it—or in spite of it.

I firmly believe the nature of life is to explore. The world is a far more magical place than we give it credit for, full of lots of possibilities if we are willing to get out there and discover them. Most of my leadership journey has been relatively unpredictable and filled with the potential for failure. Perhaps yours has, too. But I can also say it has been one of the most exciting and rewarding parts of my life.

The journey of leadership can and should be like this: an adventure borne out of hope and expectation, not fear and uncertainty. So don't get too comfortable here. "There" awaits. All you have to do is start exploring the roads.

When a motorcycle sits idle for too long, the battery dies, the brake calipers seize up, and the carburetor fills with a varnish-like sludge. The bike isn't worthless, but it's certainly *worth less* than when it's finely tuned. It has what bikers call "barn disease," and this condition is just as likely to infect a leader who doesn't explore the roads as it is a bike that sits for too long in the barn.

I want you to avoid barn disease. So I'm ending each chapter with a short review and some reflective questions that should help you apply what you're learning. Use these to grow as a leader who looks through the turn—who makes the most of the road ahead and enjoys the journey.

The Road Ahead

REVIEW

As you come upon the next "new road" in your leadership journey, keep these four best practices in mind:

- Identify your fears.
- Trust your instincts and experiences.
- Learn everything you can.
- Practice reciprocity.

REFLECT

- What kind of leader are you, a called leader or an accidental leader? Have you always felt a strong call to lead, even if it's sometimes uncomfortable? Or are you in a leadership position more because it was thrust upon you?
- Think of a time when you've felt unprepared, unqualified, or unsure about taking on a leadership challenge. How did you respond well, and how might you have improved in your response?
- What fears have prevented you from tackling a new leadership challenge?

CHAPTER 2

Scrap the Map

My husband and I love nothing more than planning a trip, especially when motorcycles are involved. We'll sit at our kitchen table with a map spread between us and trace various routes, thinking through possible road conditions, traffic, rest stops, and, of course, scenery. Then after more than enough debate and discussion, we select an initial route to follow.

One thing we've come to learn through the years is that flexibility is the name of the game on a ride. You never know how things will actually play out, and many times you need to take some different roads before reaching your destination. More often than not, these unplanned routes allow you to discover new and interesting places you hadn't expected but fully enjoyed, maybe even more so because they were serendipitous.

The unpredictability is part of the fun if you are journey-minded. Being an explorer means going to unexpected places at unexpected times in life. This is true in our leadership journey, as well. The times when we scrap the map can take us to new opportunities we hadn't planned on but that can be hugely rewarding if we remain open to the possibilities.

Rosalyn Sussman Yalow, for instance, followed a nontraditional road for women in the sciences that led her to a Nobel Prize. Yalow realized early in life that she wouldn't follow a predictable path in life. Her family encouraged her to become an elementary schoolteacher, a common career track for women who grew up in the 1920s and 1930s. But Yalow dreamed of the sciences, so she took a job as a secretary for a team of biochemists at Columbia University. She was studying stenography and might never have donned a lab coat if not for the outbreak of World War II.

With thousands of men called into the military, several universities began offering opportunities to women. Yalow accepted a teaching assistantship at the University of Illinois and became the only woman in a department of about 400 people. She earned a PhD in physics around the time the war came to a close, and hoped to become a professor or researcher: but, again, those jobs seldom went to women in those days. So she landed a job at the Bronx Veterans Administration Medical Center, where she earned laboratory space and a small salary as a consultant in nuclear physics.

This detour, however, allowed her to join forces with a young doctor at the hospital, Solomon Berson. After nearly a decade of working together, they developed radioimmunoassay (RIA), an ingenious application of nuclear physics in clinical medicine to measure the concentration of countless varieties of hormones, viruses, and chemicals. RIA changed the lives of people with diabetes and hormone-related health problems, it was a catalyst to new knowledge and thinking in every aspect of medicine, and it was used in thousands of laboratories in the United States and abroad.

In 1977, Yalow became a cowinner of the Nobel Prize in Physiology or Medicine for her work in the development of the RIA technique. She was only the second American woman to be awarded the Nobel Prize in Physiology or Medicine.

Yalow scrapped the map and changed the world. Had she not been detoured from her path to academics or traditional research positions, she most certainly would not have ended up in the right environment and with the right kind of research partner to enable the development of RIA. By embracing the path she found herself on, she discovered opportunities she otherwise never would have gotten. Her change in direction led her to a new destination few ever dream of—and a Nobel Prize—especially for a female scientist in the mid-twentieth century.

Rosalyn Yalow is an example of someone willing to scrap the map and find a new destination. She illustrates that success often comes from adapting to the path that's put beneath your feet.

My Detour from the Predictable

My early professional journey also was rerouted onto what seemed the least likely path to success. Little did I know it would become the chance of a lifetime—if I could bring myself to embrace it. And frankly, embracing it was one of the most difficult struggles of my life.

The first 10 years of my career followed a relatively predictable road. There were turns, of course, but they were clearly marked. I always saw them coming, and I always knew where they would take me. I had plugged a destination into my career GPS, and I was following the prescribed route.

I graduated from college and had a single-minded focus to build a successful career in public relations. I worked in three different advertising and public relations agencies, experienced a short stint at a city tourist attraction, transitioned into corporate life, and went back to school at night to get a master's degree.

I loved the fast pace of the industry, especially in the urban environments of Nashville and Memphis. My success made me hungrier for bigger opportunities. I wanted to climb the corporate ladder and take on greater responsibilities within a large organization, advancing as quickly as possible. Someday I would lead a communications team for a global company, or if I moved back into agency life, perhaps I would run a major office of a national public relations firm. That was my destination.

Then came the detour. At the same time that I was building my career, Raye was working hard to complete his medical training, which included medical school, residency, and a fellowship. When the time came for us to decide where he would practice, he chose an orthopedics group in the faraway northwest corner of Arkansas. Of all the choices we had, this was the one he wanted.

I was heartbroken, and I didn't give in easily or gracefully. But I moved to Arkansas, and in doing so I eventually realized one of the most important lessons in my leadership journey: the rocky detours that take us off our plan are far more valuable to our long-term success than the paved highways.

The End of the Earth?

Raye and I moved to Fayetteville, Arkansas, in the spring of 1995 after he had finished 10 years of medical training to become an orthopedic surgeon. It was a quaint college town with fewer than 75,000 residents at the time, the home of the University of Arkansas, and several small businesses, but that was about it. Former Razorbacks football coach Lou Holtz once famously said the area isn't the end of the earth, but you can see it from there. I was inclined to agree.

It was Raye's decision, not mine, to move to this tiny region in the Boston Mountains, and I admit feeling challenged by the move. I had dreams of living someplace that would give me plenty of career opportunities, so I lobbied hard to stay in Memphis or go to another big city.

I posted a huge grid in our house that I used to rank every place we were considering based on a variety of criteria. Cities like Nashville and Knoxville had big stars next to them. Although we also looked at some smaller communities, Northwest Arkansas was never on our radar.

Then we got a call from a private practice in the area inviting us to visit. They were looking for a new partner and wondered if Raye would be interested. It took only one weekend for Raye to fall in love with the place. He had great respect for the partners, who had built a highly successful and growing practice. He also appreciated the abundant outdoor beauty of the region and the simple life a smaller community offered. It would take me several years to get to that same point, not just because I wasn't sold on where we were going, but also because of what I was leaving behind.

By this time I had enjoyed three years at Embassy Suites, which was now owned by Promus Hotels and eventually would become a part of Hilton Hotels. I had just been promoted to my dream job as director of corporate communications for all of Promus Hotels' brands (Embassy Suites, Hampton Inn, and Homewood Suites) and had the privilege of being a part of the company's spin-off and public launch on the New York Stock Exchange. It was a heady time in the lodging industry, especially for our company, which was rapidly growing its franchises for all three brands.

I was truly sad to leave an organization that was widely known for its entrepreneurial spirit and track record of innovation. Plus, we had spent nearly a decade in Memphis building our lives, friendships, and careers. Now I was being asked to leave that all behind and move someplace I was pretty sure would offer a lot less.

I thought through all the possibilities as I tried to make sense of the impending move. I could look for work in the local business community or perhaps with the local chamber of commerce. Or maybe, just maybe, this was the time to start my own agency. That seemed the most unlikely option, but the thought never left my mind.

When the day came to tell my boss I was leaving, I slid a proposal across the desk and asked if he would be my first client. To my surprise, it took him only 24 hours to say yes. It was official. I would have a business of my own. Now I simply needed to figure out what to do next.

Hitting Restart

If you haven't picked up on it by now, I was not happy to leave Memphis and move to Arkansas. I was so disappointed by this decision that Raye remembers I wouldn't speak to him for quite some time, and I actually sat outside in a lawn chair in the driveway after work for three days running to avoid talking with him. The detour that took me out of the big city and off the fast track to corporate success, however, ended up putting me on the incredibly difficult but rewarding road of entrepreneurship—well ahead of my personal schedule.

Looking back, although my destination philosophy was essential in seeing me through it all, I certainly would have enjoyed it more had I done a better job of keeping a journey perspective. On the other hand, the experience also helped me reconnect with that mindset, and I began to learn the importance of being flexible and adaptable.

Regardless of where you are in your leadership journey, you need to map out a plan for where you want to go and how you will get there. But as you travel that road, know that you'll inevitably face some detours and you may have to change destinations entirely. So keep in mind these lessons I learned when I scrapped the map and looked ahead on the road I was traveling rather than focusing on the one I thought I would travel.

1. Embrace Your Entrepreneurial Spirit

The two counties that locals refer to as Northwest Arkansas now have more than a half million people, along with many amenities you would expect from a rapidly growing area: upscale restaurants, shopping, and cultural attractions like Crystal Bridges, a world-class museum of American art.

Not surprisingly, people love to live and work in this beautiful, prosperous community, and the area's growth statistics are impressive. The region regularly ranks near the top of lists for best places in America to live and do business. It was named the fastest-growing regional economy in the United States in 2000 by the Milken Institute and is projected to be the third-fastest growing economy by 2020 behind only Austin, Texas, and Raleigh, North Carolina.[1] And *US News & World Report* ranked Fayetteville number three on its list of "Best Places to Live in the USA," behind only Denver, Colorado, and Austin, Texas.[2]

More than 1,500 vendor companies have satellite offices here to serve the largest customers that most of them have: Walmart and Sam's Club. Procter & Gamble alone has more than 200 employees working from its Fayetteville office. There also is a thriving start-up community, as well as several venture capital funds and incubators that spur entrepreneurial development, particularly around retail and the impact of technology on consumer shopping patterns and practices.

In the mid-1990s, however, Northwest Arkansas was not a place most people would have considered when founding a company. The region was really more like a string of small towns about an hour north of Fort Smith, Arkansas, the closest major city. The state capitol, Little Rock, was a nearly three-hour drive, much of it through winding mountain roads (including one highway nicknamed "the pig trail"—in honor of the university's mascot, the Razorback). You could fly in and out of Fayetteville on commuter planes, but you had to drive to Tulsa or Little Rock for something that didn't sport a propeller. The four largest towns blended together so that you couldn't tell when you were leaving one and entering another, unless it was Friday night and time for a high school football game.

On the other hand, entrepreneurial roots run deep in the region. Three giants in their respective industries were all founded here—Walmart Stores, Tyson Foods, and J.B. Hunt Transport Services. Tyson was founded in the 1930s, Walmart and J.B. Hunt were founded in the early 1960s, and all three companies conducted business with each other while each was growing to international prominence. Their amazing success stories are the stuff business students still study and many books have been written about. As they grew, the region grew with them. And so did my new company.

I knew at an early age I wanted to be an entrepreneur. I had always shown a penchant for figuring out how to make money, whether it was through the typical babysitting jobs every young girl had, from picking peaches to earn enough money to buy my brother's stereo, or from setting up a gift-wrapping station in my parents' basement to earn extra money in the days leading up to Christmas. These ventures sparked my interest in capitalism and taught me that hard work literally paid off.

But I assumed you needed to be old and wise before you could start a real company. When my opportunity came, I was neither, but that didn't stop me from taking the leap, even if I had no idea what it would really take to succeed. Good thing. Turns out, it's really hard. Entrepreneurship can suck the very life out of even the most optimistic and tenacious individual with a great business idea. But once you've tasted the freedom and rewards of entrepreneurship, it becomes an irresistible siren's song.

I've founded two companies and am on my third go-around now, taking on the role of creating a new global public relations capability for my parent company. I like to build new things. Risk, high stakes, and high expectations only sweeten the deal for me.

Being a builder puts you squarely in a leadership role. Whether you're a classic entrepreneur like me, an "intrapreneur" embedded inside a company, or someone who has simply been given an entrepreneurial assignment—rolling out a new product or opening a new market, for example—organizations need leaders with an entrepreneurial spirit.

A McKinsey study titled "How Executives Grow"[3] found the five most important developmental experiences in the life of a professional were:

- "Stepping into a new position with a large scope"
- "Turning around a business"
- "Starting a new business"
- "Leading a large, high-profile special project"
- "Working outside one's home country"

Each of these requires the entrepreneurial spirit to succeed, as well as endless fortitude and resilience to stay the course regardless of the obstacles you inevitably face.

It is a unique privilege to create something from nothing. This is the domain of the entrepreneur: bringing a big idea to life through drive, passion, and an impeccable sense of timing. But you must be willing to listen to the relentless voice in your head that says, *this needs to exist*. That voice becomes the source of inspiration that compels you to take the road less traveled, and it is the decision to take the leap that defines the entrepreneur.

Embracing this entrepreneurial spirit helped me refocus my energies and lead with an eye toward the future rather than the past.

2. Learn Wherever You Are; Apply Wherever You Go

I worked for three different agencies in the early part of my career: Dye, Van Mol & Lawrence Public Relations in Nashville; Walker & Associates in Memphis; and Sossaman/Bateman/ McCuddy, also in Memphis. At each of these firms, I was mentored by one or more of the founders and had the privilege of watching them all tirelessly build a business, create a culture, and leave a legacy that is still admired and respected by many.

On the outside it can look deceivingly easy, but overnight success stories like theirs are often the product of many years of hard work, much of their own personal wealth, and a determination to keep their eyes focused on where they want to end up—leaders willing to look through the turn. Each of these agencies had founders who gave all of this and more.

At Dye, Van Mol & Lawrence, I learned how growth comes not just because of the work you do, but because of the people the agency attracts. The dynamic leadership and amazing culture created by owners Hank Dye, John Van Mol, and Tom Lawrence was a strong pull for top talent that could have gone anywhere.

At Walker & Associates, the late Deloss Walker taught me about the finer points of serving clients, presenting effectively, and winning new business. Deloss also told me something that stuck with me for the rest of my career: enthusiasm and passion can go a long way to overcome lack of experience. Be the most enthusiastic person you know even when you don't have it all figured out, and you'll go farther faster until you do. I loved the pure optimism and determination of this philosophy, and it would serve me well when I started my own agency.

At Sossaman/Bateman/McCuddy, I watched the late Ken Sossaman's star rise to unprecedented heights in the Memphis advertising scene because of his relentless pursuit for break-through creativity and learned even more about building a business, especially from working closely with Ken to build the agency's PR competency.

Having mentors like these remarkable men gave me invaluable preparation for my entrepreneurial experience, even if my experience didn't come when and where I had expected. Looking back, I realize that in addition to their patient teaching, they each encouraged me to follow in their footsteps. I distinctly remember both Deloss and Ken telling me I would build an agency someday: I had what it took. Years later, Hank told me he had seen the same thing. What they meant by that is anyone's guess, but it was encouraging to know that people who had been there and done that believed I could too.

3. Focus on Relationships; Results Will Follow

The contract with Promus Hotels allowed me to get my one-person agency started, but obviously I needed more clients to build a company. To really make it work, I needed clients in this new land called Arkansas.

So once I got over sulking in my lawn chair, we packed our bags and I set my sights on making the very best of this move. I was determined to start by building business contacts. I had left a strong network behind, and I knew it would take time and plenty of work to start a new community for myself here. One of the first weeks in, I drove to the Fayetteville Chamber of Commerce, just off the town square, walked in, joined, and asked how I could get involved. That first encounter led to more than a decade of active service with the chamber, including two stints on the board of directors. It was a great way to make friends in the business community and begin meeting influential leaders, many of whom over time would also become clients and dear friends.

These relationships also led me to meet and work with others who were building the business infrastructure in the region. The business communities at the time were each led by their local chambers of commerce with occasional support from an overarching economic development group called the Northwest Arkansas Council, founded in 1990 to help the region grow.

There was not a lot of regional business development effort at that time, and frankly it wasn't really needed. But that soon began to change as the region began expanding, and I became a passionate advocate for economic development. I was excited to be involved in the growth of major initiatives such as Arkansas Venture Forum and Accelerate Arkansas, both of which were focused on driving the growth of knowledge-based industries in the state. I served as one of the few female leaders on the executive committee of the Northwest Arkansas Council and was a member of the advisory board of GENESIS Technology Incubator at the University of Arkansas.

In addition to business infrastructure, I saw a need for developing the strength of my own industry. I had been a member of the Public Relations Society of America since I was a young professional—many years paying my own membership fees—and I served as president of the chapter in Memphis. When we moved to Northwest Arkansas, I traveled to the closest chapter in Little Rock a few times a year. I knew that if I were ever to have my own community of like-minded professionals, we would have to start a chapter in the area. I took that project on, recruiting several other area public relations professionals in the region in early 2000 to help. By 2002, we were officially approved by the national board with a new charter and local leadership. Today the chapter boasts more than 70 members and holds regular meetings, as well as an annual awards program to honor both a Communicator and Professional of the Year.

I also was eager for friends and community involvement. I joined the fledgling Junior Service League, which eventually became a Junior League, and was active in leadership for a number of years. I joined the Fayetteville Junior Civic League several years after that and became president of this prominent local women's organization. I have met countless friends and colleagues through these organizations and am still a sustaining member in both today.

While I had walked away from the personal and professional network I had thoroughly enjoyed in Memphis, I found you can build community along any road life takes you. Wherever you go, you need a support system, even if you have to build it from scratch, and many times you do. These relationships—both the friendships and the business connections—can fuel you along the way and help you find a better path forward. No doubt these relationships can make the journey sweeter and richer.

4. Chart the Best Course You Can—and Keep on Going

Probably the biggest aha of my restart was that while you need to have an idea of how you'll reach your destination, you can't map out everything. So you chart the best course you can and keep on going no matter what detours you encounter along the way. When you are an explorer with a journey mindset, you fully anticipate that you'll end up in places you hadn't planned, but you are nimble enough to course-correct as you go.

Going to Fayetteville required a leap of faith. Taking it wasn't easy for me, but fortunately, I made the jump. Had I not, I'm not sure how we would have stayed happily married, and I may never have had the opportunity to build a company, certainly not the company I built. Looking back, I can't imagine my life without these two things: a happy marriage and successful company that have both endured through thick and thin. They are two of my greatest accomplishments.

In hindsight, I can also see how leaving Memphis challenged my destination focus. Deciding to walk away from a premier position in corporate life is not something done lightly, especially for called leaders who spend much of their time and energy working to earn just such an opportunity. The move forced me to rethink my destination philosophy and consider a journey mindset, perhaps for the first time.

I've often wondered: Had I been elbowed off the career treadmill for a reason? Was this an opportunity to spend more time with my daughter, who was only 18 months old when we moved to Fayetteville? Did the move allow me to set my sights on a new destination, one that allowed me to experience entrepreneurship and growth in my career, while also having the flexibility to be a mom?

I believe all that to be true. But entrepreneurship also required a high degree of tenacity to stay the course, especially as the course changed. I considered taking an easier path on many sleepless nights when my husband was working at the hospital and the loneliness was overwhelming, or when the burdens of entrepreneurship wouldn't let me rest. These were the times I wanted to forget my long-term goals and find a simpler road.

My destination focus would never let me give up, though, and I am often thankful that my internal drive was strong enough to keep me moving forward regardless of how I felt. At times like these, the old adage of just putting one foot in front of the other sounds like pretty sage advice. By doing so, you will get where you want to go, maybe not in record time, but you can achieve your goals by keeping your eyes focused on where you want to end up. If you're willing to merge your destination focus with a journey mindset, chances are you'll enjoy the ride a lot more, too.

The Road Ahead

REVIEW

You've probably heard the expression, "bloom where you're planted." It's good advice. You can't always control or change your circumstances, so there are times when you need to scrap the map and make the most of the situation. If you approach it with the right attitude, you'll often find the new road far more interesting and rewarding than the one you originally planned to travel. When you face the inevitable detours in life, scrap your map by doing the following:

1. Embrace your entrepreneurial spirit.
2. Learn wherever you are; apply wherever you go.
3. Focus on relationships; results will follow.
4. Chart the best course you can—and keep on going.

REFLECT

- What is the biggest detour you've faced (or are facing) in pursuit of an important destination? How did (or is) your attitude impacting your ability to enjoy your journey?
- How does an entrepreneurial spirit impact the work you do?
- What issues are you passionate about, and how can you get involved in solving challenges related to them?

CHAPTER 3

Take the Handlebars

The first time I took the handlebars of a motorcycle, my fingers tingled as the adrenaline rushed throughout my body. Whether that was nerves or excitement, I'm not sure. Probably a little of both. What would this be like? Could I do it? Would I like it? Honestly, I wasn't sure of the answers, but I was eager and determined to find out.

When Raye and I returned from our trip to the Alps, he began telling me I was meant to ride—not just on the back of his bike, but on my own. I protested at first, but eventually I agreed to sign up for the motorcycle safety course. That's all it took. The class gave me the confidence to go from protester to advocate. I couldn't wait to get back on a bike—my own bike—and feel the grips of those handlebars.

Once I was licensed, I began the search. I found myself online for several evenings in a row comparing starter bikes. Raye was enthusiastic and helpful as we considered key criteria such as seat height, weight, and handlebar and foot peg positions, not to mention looks. As I narrowed my list to the ones I wanted to test drive, I found myself drawn to three that seemed perfect for me: a Ducati Monster 695, a Moto Guzzi Breva 750, and a Kawasaki Ninja 250. Color preference: red. They're all sleek, sporty, and fast, and designed for acceleration and maneuverability, just the way I like to ride.

Raye taught me to think about this carefully. You pick a bike for a lot of reasons, but ultimately you pick a bike that suits your riding style. I ended up with the Ninja and it served me well for many years. Today I ride a Honda CBR300R, also sleek, sporty, and fast . . . and red.

So what's your style? It's a good question to ask yourself as a rider and as a leader. Whether you're a called or an accidental leader, your answer reveals a lot about who you are at your core. My preference for a fast and nimble motorcycle is indicative of how I live many other parts of my life, including how I lead. Knowing myself as well as I do, it wouldn't make sense for me to own a cruiser or a dirt bike; neither would allow me to be who I am and enjoy the type of experience I'm looking for. Likewise, I rarely if ever try to be an authoritative leader or a laissez-faire leader; neither plays to my strengths or allows me to be my best.

Being clear about your leadership style is critical if you are intent on being the most effective leader you can be. One of the worst mistakes leaders make is trying to be something they're not. It's tempting to emulate others or try to become what others want us to become. I've seen many leaders take on the behaviors of individuals they know in an attempt to be what they think is expected. For example, someone might try to be tough and heartless in a performance-oriented culture, focusing solely on financial performance or other hard metrics with little to no regard for people's feelings or individual potential. But trying to be something you're not is a waste of time for yourself and others; more often than not, any positive results are short-lived. When it's carried to the extremes, you can become a destination leader who is focused on someone else's destination, not your own.

Embracing both destination leadership and a journey mindset requires a clear sense of who you are and how you want to lead. I have learned from my experiences and from working with many great leaders that the key is to lead authentically, aligning your style with your personal values and purpose, gifts and talents. This self-awareness is something most successful leaders develop over time, and the sooner you begin defining your leadership style the better.

Sorting Through the Styles

Your leadership style is shaped by many things: your natural strengths, your personality, your communication and work styles, your values and beliefs, your competencies in key performance areas, your perspective based on your personal and professional experiences, and so on. In short, your leadership style is a reflection of your approach to guiding and mobilizing the people around you.

Since the early twentieth century, researchers have studied leaders and developed theories about style and its importance on organizational effectiveness. These researchers all label leadership styles and make arguments for how and why various styles should be used.

In 1939, Kurt Lewin was one of the earliest researchers to identify distinct styles of leadership—authoritarian, democratic, and laissez-faire. His work provided the foundation for many studies that followed.

Paul Hersey and Ken Blanchard began describing situational leadership theory in 1969. Their view was that a leader's style should change based on the needs of the moment. They identified four primary styles: telling, selling, participating, and delegating.

Servant leadership, a timeless concept, was woven into modern leadership theory by Robert Greenleaf in 1970 with his essay, "The Servant as Leader." During the same decade, Bernard M. Bass identified what is often considered the most effective style: transformational leadership, which uses a leader's ability to inspire and motivate others to action, helping the organization achieve its goals while also helping the members of the group realize their potential. Bass and others also studied the transactional style, which defines the role of the follower as one who simply fulfills tasks and assignments given to them by the leader in exchange for pay.

Daniel Goleman's "Leadership That Gets Results" was a landmark *Harvard Business Review* study published in 2000. Goleman and his colleagues studied more than 3,000 executives over three years to identify what leadership behaviors impacted company climate and financial performance. The research team grouped the behaviors into several commonly seen leadership styles including pacesetting, authoritative, affiliative, coaching, coercive, and democratic.

During that same time, another school of thought was brought forward: emotional intelligence, which relies heavily on a leader's ability to manage his or her own emotions and those of others. Goleman popularized this concept in 1995, and it is still widely used today. You often hear about someone's EQ—emotional quotient—when describing capacity for leadership.

Also during the 1990s, Ron Heifetz and Marty Linsky introduced the concept of adaptive leadership, which presents an approach for leaders to use when facing complex problems in times of uncertainty and for which there is no clear solution. Leaders must innovate in real time and engage their teams to find new answers that may challenge previously held values and beliefs.

Executive intelligence is a more recent concept and a favorite of mine. Introduced in 2006 by Justin Menkes in a book by the same title, this approach identifies three key areas in which leaders must be effective for success: tasks and the ability to solve problems, people and the ability to manage relationships with others, and a strong self-awareness and an ability to learn from one's mistakes. I like its balanced approach on tasks, others, and self, and its argument that although most leaders are good at the first two, few master all three. If we can learn to manage ourselves, we can break through to become truly exceptional leaders.

Not only are there lots of theories on leadership style, there also are plenty of assessment tools to help leaders identify and maximize their style. Among the more popular are DiSC, Myers-Briggs Type Indicator (MBTI), Clifton StrengthsFinder, and John Maxwell Leadership Assessment. Another that is lesser known but very effective is TotalSDI. All of these tools are valuable to help you reflect on those things that shape your leadership style.

Does it matter what style(s) a leader has in her repertoire? More than you might think. Surprisingly, although companies have long spent tremendous time and effort on cost-cutting and revenue-driving initiatives, Goleman's study found leadership style accounted for as much as 30 percent of an organization's bottom-line profitability. This is compelling evidence that your style matters, and being effective in your style can be a game-changer for your and your team's success.

Advice on the Grips

When I mentor or coach younger leaders, one of the first things we talk about is defining their style so they can lead authentically as they grow in their role and into future roles. Regardless of their age or their industry or any other factors that I've come across, I've found some of the advice I've gleaned from books, mentors, and experience applies universally.

Find the Authentic You

I remember wondering what kind of leader I wanted to become during my formative leadership years in the mid- to late 1990s. I had three strong mentors in my former agency bosses, but I found my touchstone in John Maxwell, an author who was writing about leadership in a very unique way at that time. Maxwell's work spoke to me profoundly. He wrote about leadership that was beyond the money, fame, and success. He was a lone voice in a Gordon Gekko era. When most of what I heard was how to win at any cost, Maxwell was spreading the leadership gospel of influence and integrity.

I accumulated many of his books—as he wrote them, I bought them—and I still have them stacked high on my bookshelf. They became my handbooks of sorts for leadership. This was the kind of leader I aspired to be: one who was successful, sure, but one who also could attain the "higher calling of leadership." I remember reading *Developing the Leader within You* and setting my sights on becoming a Pinnacle Leader, one whom others willingly choose to follow because of who the person is and what he or she represents: character, values, and stewardship of what the person has been given. This was enough of a challenge as well as a North Star that I kept it in my mind and heart during my earliest leadership experiences.

As you explore your leadership style, you may begin to feel as though you aren't precisely any one style, but rather a combination of several. Goleman's study actually showed that the most effective leaders switch between various styles as the situation demands. We all have different strengths that manifest themselves at different times, and we should constantly evolve as a leader.

I tend to prefer a collaborative and motivational style of leadership, but I have on many occasions been quite directive and pacesetting when singularly focused on achieving a goal. These preferences fit with my DiSC profile, which is D/i, also referred to as the inspirational pattern. It is common for destination leaders with a journey mindset to strive for balance between leading for results while maintaining relationships.

You might also conclude that you're not really like other leaders at all, which can be a little scary. You want to see at least some of yourself in others you know or admire. But I believe that to be the most effective leader you can be, there must be something different about you. Why? There are myriad leaders who look and feel the same. They have chosen to align their beliefs and behaviors with others or with their organizations so much so that they have lost virtually all of their individuality. In this case, who wants to follow them? There must be something compelling that makes people, whether employees, clients, or significant others, pick you.

Being different is attractive and makes you stand out from the crowd. The trick is: you must be you (unless you're a jerk, and in that case you need more than this book—consider hiring a good executive coach). If you try to be something you're not, people will recognize it pretty quickly, and there is nothing less desirable than a fake. Which begs the question: What makes you, you?

Answer: know yourself. Be sure others have a clear idea of who you are, too. Although your style(s) can change, certain things at your core never should. I believe the most authentic and effective leadership style can be drawn from a combination of timeless attributes and beliefs including:

- Your gifts and talents—what you are naturally good at
- Your values—what you believe is most important, possibly also including your faith
- Your purpose—why you are here and what you want your life's work to be about

You have the opportunity to lead at your best when you are clear about these things and can act in a way that authentically and consistently reflects who you are. You can bring that to life in all sorts of ways: in what you say, how you make decisions, and the manner in which you carry yourself around others in both good times and bad.

As I grow, I don't fundamentally change who I am, my values, or my leadership philosophy in the process. This is who I am. To attempt to become someone drastically different would not be authentic. Embracing who you are as a leader makes the journey far more enjoyable, even if you discover that you are not a fit for every situation.

People Follow People, not Titles

My good friend Wendy Davidson is a role model for many leaders, including myself, because of her ability to lead authentically. She has spent much of her career blazing a trail for other female leaders to follow, mostly by succeeding in the male-dominated food industry.

Learning to lead comfortably in her own skin helped Wendy rise through the ranks during a 16-year career with Tyson Foods, where she eventually served in several senior vice president roles. She went on from Tyson to hold two senior leadership roles at McCormick. She's been president of Kellogg's U.S. specialty channels in North America since 2013 and also is a member of the company's Global Leadership Team.

Wendy learned early in her career that she needed to spend time with people, especially people on the front lines, so they could get to know her, because a relationship built on transparency resulted in respect and trust.

"They need to know the person I am and why I make the decisions I do, not just what the decision is," she told me one morning when we were talking about leadership styles. "So letting people in was a way of allowing me to learn but also to lead."

For example, anyone who has ever worked with, for, or around Wendy learns quickly that she values her family. Why? Because she is proactive and intentional about sharing that value.

"I engage the team and their families if I can with my family," she told me. "Family is a huge part of my life, and I need my team to know that."

Wendy doesn't just talk about her family, she listens and learns about the families of the people she works with. She leads by example when it comes to prioritizing family. People see it in her work schedule since her children are younger. Many days she doesn't get to the office until 8:30 so she can see the children off to school, and she makes time to attend important school events—all without sacrificing the quality of her work.

Be Comfortable Being You

When we first step into leadership roles, we often don't have a clear idea of what it means to be the boss. We have stereotypes in our minds or we simply emulate what we've seen others do. Rarely do we have the confidence to simply be ourselves.

"When you're in your first leadership role, you just don't know how to act," Wendy told me. "So you rely on what you see in other leaders, what you read in books, or, quite honestly, what you saw in movies or on TV."

You might learn something from those sources, but they won't provide the precise formula for your success as a leader.

As Wendy points out, "It has to be what works for you and those you lead."

That requires vulnerability. You have to take the risk of opening yourself up to others, which, ironically, empowers your team. It doesn't show weakness; it shows your strength.

Wendy recalled how challenging it was to show vulnerability early in her career when she felt her youth and her gender worked against her.

"If I showed any weakness, then I felt it would validate somebody thinking that I got the job simply because I was female or that I wasn't qualified to be in the role," she said. "It took several mentors who said things like, 'Wendy, there's a reason we put you in this role and it wasn't because you were female and it wasn't because you were young, it's because of what we knew you could do in that role. So do it the way you can uniquely do that, and you'll be successful.'"

Wendy began developing her own leadership style based on who she was, but that's not a one-and-done process. It's never-ending. In fact, one of Wendy's most insightful learning periods came when she took a year off after leaving Tyson Foods. She was a senior vice president at the time, so you might wonder what more she could learn about herself as a leader. But the year away from work—what she called her "forced sabbatical" because of her noncompete clause with Tyson—allowed her to develop fresh insights about herself.

"It was an enormous gift," she said. "It gave me the chance to really explore who I was as a person, as a leader, as a wife, as a mother, as a friend. During that year, I had to be comfortable with just being Wendy."

This was driven home for her when she joined two boards and found herself with no title to attach to her name during the introductions at her first meetings.

"I said something like, 'I'm Wendy Davidson of the David-sons,'" she said. "Everyone laughed to ease the awkwardness I felt, and the whole rest of the day I thought: Is that enough? Is Wendy Davidson enough? They all knew I was no longer employed, but what I didn't know was why they wanted me on the board. It wasn't my company or my title. It was just me. It was incredibly empowering. So during that year I really explored what parts of me I wanted to keep and what parts of myself I wanted to refine, and to know that wherever I came out on the other end, Wendy Davidson was enough."

From this important time of introspection, Wendy moved on to McCormick and then Kellogg, wiser and more certain of the leader she was and wanted to continue becoming as she grew in her career.

Listen, Learn, and Repeat

The best leaders have an accurate picture of their true strengths and how they are perceived by others. Some of this, of course, comes through formal performance reviews and 360 assessments, but much of it comes during the daily course of life when people provide feedback on the fly. They might voluntarily provide it, or you might need to ask (and then probe more deeply into the answers).

Mentors are particularly helpful in this regard, but they don't have to work in your organization or even in your industry to provide useful insights. Some of the best feedback can come from those who know you well but who might be much more removed from your day-to-day leadership.

Wendy advocates building a personal board of directors, something she learned at a Women's Foodservice Forum event, and filling it with a diverse group of people. Your board could include someone in a position you aspire to be in, someone in other parts of the industry that are unfamiliar to you, someone in a totally different industry, and someone who can feed your spirit by helping you in your faith journey.

"These are people who know you personally, so they know what makes you tick, and they are also people who will be brutally honest," Wendy said. "I made a list of people and asked for their help as I continued on my own developmental journey. Everyone I asked said yes and told me they were honored."

Too many young leaders don't ask for advice, she said, because they don't realize, as Wendy puts it, that "asking is a gift you're giving somebody; you're saying, 'You have something that I can learn from and I'd like you to be a part of my moving forward.'" Giving a person the gift of asking for his or her help allows that person to give you the gift of helping you grow as a leader.

"To this day," Wendy said, "I make a point of reaching back to those people and saying thank you for the gift that they gave me in feedback. They are a part of my journey."

Wendy plays an important role in the journey of many other leaders, too. Not only is she on my personal board of directors, but she mentors countless others and is the 2016 chairman of the Women's Foodservice Forum board.

Find Your Passion in Your Work

Authentic leadership stems from doing what we love. If you aren't passionate about your work, it will show. This doesn't mean you're passionate about every task and assignment. Maybe you aren't passionate about filling out an expense report, right?

But part of finding your leadership style is finding your passions and how they connect with the work that you do, because the people around you will feed off your passions, regardless of how your personal style expresses them.

When other people see your passion in your leadership style, they are naturally encouraged to find it in their own approach to work, which, of course, makes them happier and more productive.

"I need my team to know what powers me and that they should find what powers them, as well," Wendy said. "If people aren't happy in what they are doing, I'd rather they'd be willing to say, 'This is not filling my cup. Can we find a place where I can channel my passions into something that is useful for the company, and that the company can get the very best of me?'"

Wendy recalled two people in particular on a team she led who, in her opinion, could do more than they were doing in their roles. She sat down with them at different times and told them so.

"One, I encouraged to go back to school, and she went on to become a regional sales manager," she said. "Another went on to lead supply chain and our sales and operations process for a division. She actually set the forecast accuracy standard for our company. Both needed someone to say, 'I see something in you that maybe you don't see in yourself and I'm going to invest in that.' Which, when I look back, is exactly what my mentors did for me. They said, 'I see something in you. I'm going to challenge you, and I've got your back.'"

When you are clear about what fuels you as a leader, you can give that gift to others and coach and mentor them to lead in the same manner.

The Balancing Act

Destination leaders are focused on their goals, of course, but that doesn't mean they don't love their work. Many of them are passionate about their work and drawn to it—as I can personally attest.

When I was young, one of the people in my life I most wanted to please was my mother. So as I thought about my career options, I naturally sought her opinion.

"What do you want me to be?" I asked her.

Mom's response was so typical of her.

"Happy," she said with a smile.

She didn't care if I made all the money in the world. My mother wanted me to find work that brought me joy and that allowed me to live out my passions. Her freeing response led me, a hard-charging destination leader, toward public relations, a field I felt passionate about, rather than becoming a lawyer or entering another more commonly known and respected profession.

The old adage is true: if you love what you do, you'll never work a day in your life. There is great wisdom in that, and we can role model it for our children, as well as for our employees. Finding passion in what we do is a big part of how we enjoy the ride of our work and of our lives. The trick is finding the balance of loving what we do and spending time on it, while loving other aspects of our lives and spending time on those things, including families, friends, and hobbies.

As you'll learn later in this book, this didn't always come easily for me. I know it's a struggle for other destination leaders. The intersection of "destination and journey" is clearly evident in the struggle to choose how you will lead, particularly in the amount of time you spend focusing on your work. This is part of leadership style—the intensity you have and the importance of work in your overall life says a lot about the type of leader you are.

But balance also comes because we are being true to ourselves and leading authentically. Our style aligns with our gifts and talents, our values, and our purpose.

What's your style? Do you dare to be yourself, or are you still trying to fit into a mold someone else has cast for you? When you find the courage and the freedom to be who you really are as a leader, you will find those who want to follow you because of your honesty and your transparency. This is the path to becoming a Pinnacle Leader, one who others willingly choose to follow because of who you are and what you represent.

It's also the way forward to becoming the most effective leader you can be.

The Road Ahead

REVIEW

Authenticity is critical to a leader's success, especially for those of us who want to combine destination leadership with a journey mindset.

- Find the authentic you.
- People follow people, not titles.
- Be comfortable being you.
- Listen, learn, and repeat.
- Find your passion in your work.

REFLECT

Think through your leadership style and how you feel about it by answering these questions:

- What are your gifts and talents—what are you naturally good at?
- What are your values—what do you believe is most important?
- What is your purpose—why are you here and what do you want your life's work to be about?

CHAPTER 4

Slipstreaming

One of the ironic aspects of motorcycling is that it's a solitary adventure that typically plays out in groups. There's safety in numbers and a camaraderie in sharing the road and the destinations with people you love. You learn to ride as a team, with each rider playing different roles at different times.

Motorcyclists, for instance, often take advantage of the slipstream—the area of reduced air pressure just behind a fast-moving vehicle. A leader gets out front and allows others to draft behind her, thereby conserving fuel by driving against less resistance.

In business, a leader willingly rides in the front, showing the way, and allowing others to draft and follow, until the time is right for others to go forward on their own. This can present a challenge because it means giving up control, empowering others to succeed, and to be blunt, getting out of the way. But it's the best way to move an organization forward, because it allows everyone in the group to do their part and to enjoy the journey.

When I began my company, I rode out front—alone. Very soon, however, I learned the importance of riding with others, that is, of attracting and keeping diverse talent, building effective teams, creating unique talent solutions for challenging problems, and designing efficient labor strategies. In fact, the company didn't take off until we had wonderful people at the table with me. If you look at the growth of Mitchell, we always benefitted from having the right team in place at different points along the way. My name was on the door, but it was far more than just me making Mitchell a success.

As a leader, you want to blaze a path into an exciting future. But getting to that destination is much more challenging and much less rewarding if you try to do it on your own. You need other people. Building and leading great teams not only was central to our organizational success, but the relationships made each stretch of the journey more meaningful as we progressed toward each new destination.

My Talent War

In the early years of building Mitchell, I faced an unusual challenge. While my competitors in big cities were immersed in the "war for talent," I didn't have enough soldiers to even get into the fight in the first place.

The best and the brightest public relations talent tended to gravitate toward major metro areas: they weren't looking to move to a smaller market like Northwest Arkansas. Not surprisingly, in the early years of my company, there was a shortage of talent in the region.

That's not to say there weren't skilled public relations professionals locally, but most of them worked for my clients. I valued the trust we shared so much that I made a commitment, to them and to myself, not to hire my clients' talent. I had to find another way to recruit the people I needed to support our workload and the agency's growth.

My solution: hire the best people I could find regardless of where they were. Mitchell was winning national assignments, so where my team lived was of little consequence. I had proven you could live and work anywhere if you had the knowledge, expertise, and availability to meet your clients' needs. Now I just needed to expand that model.

In our first 10 years, I established a network that grew to 12 senior-level professionals—all women—who lived around the country and regularly worked for me. These were friends or colleagues I knew in the industry, or they were referrals from trusted sources. Some had previously worked full-time for multinational public relations agencies, which were our largest competitors; others had worked in-house for major corporations, media outlets, or marketing firms.

Nearly everyone had an impressive pedigree and a killer résumé. For one reason or another, however, they had chosen to leave their full-time jobs. Some were staying home with their children; others were trailing spouses and had moved where their husband had taken a job. Still others had decided to start their own part-time consulting practice.

It turned out their decision to leave the fast-track was a growing trend. I found myself benefiting from the early stages of the "freelance economy." The Bureau of Labor Statistics indicated approximately 9 million people in the United States were officially "self-employed" in 1995, and the number is more than 15 million today.[1] The percentage of self-employed Americans has held steady in the 10 to 12 percent range for roughly 30 years. But a 2015 report by the Freelancers Union and Upwork (an online freelancing platform) estimated that nearly 54 million workers—about a third of the U.S. workforce—did some type of freelance work in the past year. That number, of course, included people who were moonlighting, were temporary employees, or combined freelancing with traditional work.[2]

I didn't know my workforce strategy was on the front end of such a trend when I was starting my agency. I just knew their employers' loss was my gain: incredible talent was becoming more available on a national level, but only for flexible work assignments, which was exactly what I could offer them. This dream team got us around the huge obstacle we faced as a growing professional service company. It met the needs of our clients, as well as the needs of these professionals who wanted to work part-time.

As the team grew, we used a buddy system to help those who were newer learn from those who had been around longer. We worked closely as a group, connecting through conference calls and email.

Our normal workflow process looked something like this: I would walk the halls several days a week in the corporate offices of our biggest clients—Walmart, Tyson Foods, and J.B. Hunt—meeting with key contacts and bringing back as many assignments as I could get. I'd sort through them, devise a strategy, develop a work plan and general timeline, and begin thinking through who on the team was right to work with me on a project. Then I'd see who was interested and available. I spent many a Sunday afternoon calling each member of the team to check in on them: how they were doing, how their kids were, whether they felt good about the work I'd been giving them, and what their availability was.

Certain times of the year were a bigger challenge than others. In the summer, several members of my team focused full-time on their school-aged children who were home. While that was a great benefit to them as subcontractors, it meant much of the work fell on whoever else was available. Often, it simply fell to me. So I spent many summers carrying the workload of valued team members whom I knew I'd have back in the fall. I just did the best I could to keep all the balls in the air until they returned.

Despite the unpredictability of my virtual labor model, it worked extremely well. I could offer our clients senior-level professionals with deep expertise and knowledge about public relations and related disciplines. My all-star team allowed me to scale; I could say "yes" to more and more engagements from clients and continue growing the business. I had more brains than my own to help me think through strategy and campaign ideas. I enjoyed working with other people, and this gave me an opportunity to develop new skills as a leader of a very collaborative and creative team.

By the early 2000s, the virtual team was hitting its stride and my local talent pool was beginning to grow, too. As new talent moved into the market, I snapped it up as quickly as possible.

Those of us who were nearby got together fairly frequently, once a month or more, but it was hard on those who lived farther away to feel connected to the team. So I started flying everyone in for an annual agency retreat and team celebration. We reviewed our accomplishments, planned for the coming year, and then enjoyed an outing. One year we had cooking lessons and a gourmet meal by a local chef. Another year we did a spa night.

Each time we gathered, friendships grew stronger, colleagues learned from each other, and we marveled at how unique and effective the team was. We were proving that high-performing teams didn't have to be clustered in a single office, or even in a single city or state. We were spread around the country, everyone working from home offices, yet we were working with some of the world's finest corporations, doing national work that we were winning away from highly respected traditional agencies.

I made my first full-time hire in 2005, bringing Michael Clark on as my number two, but we kept the virtual network intact even as we created more full-time positions. We simply created a hybrid labor model that was incredibly flexible by design, comprising both full-time and part-time team members.

The model helped the agency, as well as the team. People moved from one status to the other, depending upon what was going on in their lives. Several who'd stayed home while their children were young transitioned to full-time work when their children went to school. One full-time employee scaled back to part-time while going through a divorce. Others moved to part-time when they followed spouses to new jobs in other cities. The beauty of the network is it allowed the agency to retain the talent but gave people options about when, how much, and where they worked.

We've grown the Mitchell team over the last 20 years to more than 70 full-time employees in three offices—Fayetteville, New York, and Chicago. Yet we've kept the virtual network, now called LocalLink, which includes more than 40 professionals in 14 states. It's no longer just public relations pros. It now includes videographers, photographers, researchers, graphic designers, and social media experts.

LocalLink gives us a presence in all corners of the country when we need boots on the ground for client events or other activities. It brings invaluable local market knowledge to our team. It also offers us "surge capacity," since these workers help us handle overflow work when our full-time team is booked solid. This means we can still help clients with whatever needs they have regardless of how busy our full-time team is. Because we pay those team members only for the hours or the projects they agree to, the agency has greater flexibility with our labor dollars and, at times, higher profitability.

Depending upon your business needs, this is a model that could help you manage capacity and work flow more efficiently. Full-time employees are best for steady, predictable work. Part-time employees are ideal for work that ebbs and flows. Just be sure you observe any IRS rules or other employment-related regulations.

Making Great Teams

I learned a lot by leading a virtual team. I also learned a lot as the company grew and more of our team worked together under the same roof. And I learned a great deal from several mentors who shared their wisdom with me.

Perhaps the first and most fundamental lesson was how important it was to have a strong and capable team in place—no matter where they were located—to help grow the business, especially for a professional services company that depends on people for its capacity. Simply "having" a team isn't enough, of course. The team has to work well together and produce great results, or it will struggle to reach its destination, much less enjoy the journey along the way.

Here are a few important lessons I have learned for building effective teams, not only from my own experience but also from the experiences of others.

Find a Common Purpose

Mike Duke, the CEO of Walmart from 2009 to 2014, has been one of the most influential mentors in my leadership journey at Mitchell. Over the course of a 15-year friendship, he has challenged me to grow a better business and become a better leader. One of the things I've always admired was his ability to recruit and mobilize talent into high-functioning teams.

Mike is best known for his time at Walmart, but his well-rounded career began in Atlanta when he was hired out of Georgia Tech to help Rich's Department Store with a discount spin-off called Richway. Macy's purchased that company, and he worked for them in several capacities—in human resources, store operations, logistics, real estate—for 20 years before joining Walmart. He worked in logistics and later was president of Walmart US and then led Walmart International as a vice chairman of the company.

In November 2008, with the world in the middle of the Great Recession, the board of directors of Walmart asked Mike to replace the retiring Lee Scott in the coming year as the company's CEO, the team leader of roughly 2.1 million associates around the world. One of the first things he leaned on, for himself and for the teams around him, was the purpose Sam Walton had in mind when he founded the company in 1962: to help people save money and live better.

"Many ingredients go into making a really great team," Mike told me during a recent visit as we talked about recruiting talent and building a team, "but it probably starts with a common purpose, a common mission that all the members of the team really share in. It's what they are going to achieve as a team."

The purpose typically centers on shared values and the team culture, which are why those elements are so important to building any successful organization. They are discussed in more depth in Chapter 6, but for now it's important to remember that shared values drive a positive organizational culture and allow teams to rally around a common purpose.

Embrace Selflessness

Legendary UCLA basketball coach John Wooden once said, "The main ingredient of stardom is the rest of the team."[3]

Great teams are in it for each other, not just for their individual success. When the team wins, it's more rewarding and enjoyable for everyone. You see this in sports all the time. Great teams typically have great players, and the superstars often are called on to make key plays at key times. But they win championships by playing together.

Consider the NBA, a league filled with individual superstars. Michael Jordan and LeBron James, two of the greatest individual players in history, didn't win championships until they had the right combination of players and coaches around them. Mild-mannered players like David Robinson and Tim Duncan qualified as stars for San Antonio teams that were best known for their team defense while winning five titles between 1999 and 2015.

"Probably the greatest player in the game right now is focused on assisting other players and the ball movement of the team rather than his individual points, and I think it applies that way in business," Mike told me. "You can have a very talented individual player. There's a lot to be said for that, of course. But how does that individual player complement the whole team? Provide the assist and create the environment where every player performs to their fullest potential?"

Discover Diversity

I've spent much of my career looking for ways to champion the value of women in the workplace. Hiring more people who were overlooked in years past, and paying them fairly, is the right thing to do for anyone with any sense of social and moral justice. But team diversity isn't just about hiring more women, or more people of color, or more of any one thing. It's about inclusion and discovering what you *and* your team can gain from anyone with different experiences, different insights, different backgrounds, and different skills.

Abraham Lincoln provides a great example. The sixteenth president of the United States guided the country through what perhaps was the most turbulent time in its history, and you might think the key to his leadership success was pulling together a team of talented and like-minded colleagues to help shape and shepherd his vision. But you'd be only half right. Lincoln leaned heavily on talented people, but as acclaimed historian Doris Kearns Goodwin points out, he also brought "disgruntled opponents together to create the most unusual cabinet in history."[4]

Goodwin, author of the bestselling book *Team of Rivals* about Lincoln's presidency, points out Lincoln's cabinet consisted of strong-willed, opinionated people, many of them his opponents. It took a skilled and confident leader to manage such a team. Lincoln had to know when to listen and when to end the debate and make his own decisions. He had to know when and how to share credit, as well as when and how to hold people accountable. He also had to know how to do so in ways that kept the spirit and vitality of that team alive and thriving.

I'm inspired by his team-building strategy and can't help but think he got better results because of his bold approach to build a team of leaders who brought diverse points of view. As leaders, we too have to develop the emotional intelligence, strength, and wisdom to assemble and lead the best teams for whatever challenge our organizations face, and diverse thinking will get us there faster.

Mike's role in leading Walmart International during a time of global expansion for the company drove home for him the importance of diversity and the strength a company can gain by using the knowledge and skills of teams from different cultures. Not only did the company share its expertise as it expanded internationally, but also the U.S. operations became stronger by learning from its counterparts in other parts of the world.

One of Mike's greatest legacies as a leader was his emphasis on opening doors for women at the top level of Walmart. He saw it not just as the right thing to do for people, but also the right thing to do for the business. Women represent a huge percentage of the customer base for any retailer, not to mention a high percentage of the frontline workforce. So it made good business sense to give them a seat at the leadership table to help shape the direction and policies of the company. But Mike's commitment wasn't just to hire a more diverse workforce, it was also to set them up for success.

"If you love people and you want to see all people succeed, you establish an environment where every person plays to their fullest potential," he said, "then create an environment where people don't feel constrained, where they feel they can contribute. And I think when every person—every man, every women—can perform to their fullest . . . well, that's the right thing to do, and it's really better for the business."

One of the ways Mike did that was by creating the Global Council of Women Leaders at Walmart to give them a forum to share their views and grow professionally.

"It was the most senior leaders from around the world," Mike said. "They were international leaders from South Africa, from the United Kingdom, from the United States. They would come with different ideas about women's roles and contributions that they could make to the company. It was a great learning experience for me, and it made the company better, of course, too."

Mike also oversaw the establishment of Walmart's Global Women's Economic Empowerment Initiative in 2011, which works to create development and advancement opportunities for Walmart's associates around the world and economic opportunity for people and businesses along the company's supply chain, including women-owned small businesses and diverse suppliers.

Fill Your Gaps

A diverse team needs skills that complement each other, or else it will find work frustrating and inefficient. That's why it's so important to hire for your weaknesses. You want people on your team who can shore up the functions that you don't really love or have the expertise to handle well.

For instance, Marla Hunt was a key member of my virtual network during our early years. All teams need good processes that keep the work and the ideas flowing. Marla's knack for operations was something we really needed. She helped devise many of the systems and practices we used during that time and for several years afterward as the company grew beyond the virtual network.

Getting Marla for what ended up being 10 years (and she eventually did become a full-time employee) was an important win, not just for me but for the company. We complemented each other nicely, because my interests were much more oriented toward the *who* and the *what* of our work, not the *how*. Marla kept things running behind the scenes, managing operations and helping with the finances and HR tasks, freeing me to spend more time with clients and the team, thinking about the business and how we could continue to grow it.

Plant in Fertile Ground

When Mike was a young leader, he found himself in charge of an underperforming team.

"I thought the answer was for me to work more hours," he told me. "If I can just put in more time, if I can work harder as the team leader, then I would set the example."

His plan wasn't working. Fortunately, Mike was open to constructive criticism, and one of his team members pulled him aside to encourage him to empower her and the other team members rather than trying to do so much of the work himself. He needed to practice slipstreaming as a leader, setting the pace and the direction for the team but at times allowing others to take the lead, too.

"I began to understand what leadership really is," Mike said. "It's not about the leader working more hours, working harder, faster, or contributing more. We ended up with a very successful outcome, but we had to fall a few points behind before we came back and became a winning team."

Mike allowed a colleague to give him honest feedback on what he needed to do differently for the team to get back on track. He also listened and made necessary changes. This is another example of a learning leader: he is open and willing to listen to feedback from others, and adapt and improve as he goes. It's a key way leaders create a fertile field in which a team can grow and develop.

"I can recall years ago when I first went to Walmart International, leaders in one of the overseas markets were telling me how some of the merchandise that was coming from the United States wasn't best for their local market," Mike said. "I listened and went in the store and could see that the local customer didn't have an interest in that particular item."

Mike began giving local leaders greater authority over the merchandise they carried, and their sales improved as they became more local.

"So I think that goes all the way up through an organization," Mike said. "Be really good listeners, and reinforce an open-minded willingness to try, a willingness to even make mistakes."

At Mitchell, I sought to build what Jack Welch, then CEO of GE, had labeled a "boundaryless"[5] organization—one that encouraged collaboration and information-sharing across the team. I not only kept regular communication flowing from me to the team, I also empowered the team to talk to each other and to clients. These were incredibly talented individuals. I wanted them to enjoy what they did and to bring their best thinking forward. A collaborative and empowering culture was what it would take to help us win.

I've found that leaders of good teams know how to ask the right questions to stimulate thinking among their teams. They don't just go in and tell them what to do; they engage their teams in thinking through challenges and opportunities together. Better solutions come from teams who work through things together rather than one person coming up with a solution on their own.

That was Mike's approach with the groups he mentored.

"People would expect me to come in with a speech and that I would do a lot of talking," he said. "That was never the case. I would always go in with a few questions. It wouldn't take very many to stimulate ideas and discussion. As the CEO of Walmart, it's not really about giving a lot of direction. It's really more about listening, developing, and allowing the organization to expand."

Leaders who really listen and empower their teams not only build great teams, but also mold better leaders for their organization and get better business results. Too many leaders still want to build a team and tell it what to do. But that command-and-control style of leadership breeds bureaucracy and slowness, and it discourages innovation and entrepreneurial thinking. The disruptive nature of business today and the changing attitudes and expectations of the workforce have combined to make this style of leadership virtually obsolete. The world rewards adaptive leaders who assess challenges quickly and engage teams to manage through change together in real time.

When teams are planted in fertile ground, they feel the freedom to communicate not only up and down in an organization, but diagonally. They are driven by their common purpose. They value what they have to offer and what they can learn from others, wherever in the organizations those "others" might be.

This requires team leaders to set aside their egos and shift their understanding about their role. It's not to come up with every idea or have all the answers; it's about getting the best from their teams. It takes maturity and the wisdom that comes through age and experience before many of us who are destination leaders can embrace this philosophy. We are so driven to achieve our goals that we want to push ourselves and others to reach them. Journey-minded leaders are willing to invite others to join them in setting and reaching goals. Then they are willing to help them succeed.

"I never spend a lot of time thinking about legacy," Mike told me. "But I can remember about 20 years ago I got promoted and moved from Washington DC to Missouri. When I left Washington, there was a going-away party because in my promotion, nine other people were able to be promoted. These nine people had a dinner and said, 'We're so happy you got promoted.' It allowed nine other people to move up through the ripple effect of succession and development."

Mike had led in a way that prepared many others for leadership when the opportunity arose. That's a legacy born from planting teams in fertile ground.

Attracting Great Talent

The war for talent can seem like a never-ending battle. More and more jobs require a specialized set of skills. Top talent, especially millennials, often expect more than just a paycheck from their employer. They want a great culture, great benefits, and a "purpose" in the business that serves the greater good.

One of the many studies that back this up was a simple, three-question survey in 2014 by CollegeFeed, an online career site that's now owned by AfterCollege. Most of the 15,000 millennials who responded to the survey were still in college, and the rest were recent grads. One of the three questions was, "What are the top three things you look for when considering an employer?" The top response was "people and culture fit," followed by "career potential," and "work/life balance." Compensation, while important, still ranked fourth.

Sanjeev Agrawal, the CEO of CollegeFeed at the time of the study, said the data left him with one key takeaway: "It is imperative to focus on communicating your culture and career growth to potential employees. The two fundamental questions that young job seekers ask, and that companies need to answer, are: 'What is it like to work there?' and 'What kind of growth can I expect?'"[6]

So if you want to attract top talent, you can start by doing all the things we just talked about in the previous section:

build teams that find a common purpose, embrace selflessness, discover diversity, fill your gaps, and plant in fertile ground. Talented people will want to join those types of teams and work in those types of environment.

That's part of creating a great culture, of course, and again, we'll talk in more detail on creating a great culture in a later chapter. But remember, the talent you want to attract has to be people who share your values and improve your culture. Otherwise, they become part of the problem, not part of the solution.

Finding "best-fit talent" starts with spending time on it as a leader. We have to commit to recruiting, watching for great talent, and cultivating relationships with exceptional people when we meet them. They might not come to us immediately, but over time, people are more likely to be drawn to us when timing and opportunity align, if we've built a relationship with them along the way.

Some of the best people are not looking for a change, but they are willing to make a change if they connect with you and buy into your culture, vision, and values.

"The best talent I recruited in my time in leadership was people who weren't looking to make a change," Mike told me. "I recruited them by just asking questions and talking and building relationships with them over time."

Another important way leaders can attract talent is to offer opportunities for development so they can do more than just a job; they can also grow as a professional while they are on your team. This includes formal programs, but they also want to see a leader who models development, who never stops learning and growing, and who helps everyone around her learn and grow.

Many of the leadership practices Mike put into place at Walmart are timeless lessons for leaders of teams large and small. By watching Mike and many others, I learned how to build effective, diverse teams that shared a common purpose. I saw the value of being more about the team than about yourself and how to encourage and empower others to grow and develop, too. I absolutely understood the importance of cultivating relationships with people no matter when I met them so that over time I would be able to attract the best and brightest talent to our team when the opportunity was there.

These lessons served me well and helped me grow Mitchell in the early years—the first 10 years, from 1995 to 2005. Together with my virtual team, we laid a strong foundation for the company that would allow it to grow in the future. I could not have foreseen what was around the next turn for the agency, but I knew that with world-class clients like Walmart, Tyson, and J.B. Hunt and some of the industry's best professionals on my team, we were operating on all cylinders and ready to move to a higher gear.

Good thing, because what came next was the ride of our lives.

The Road Ahead

REVIEW

The best leaders know the importance of teams, not just because they help get things done but because they can make the journey more meaningful—for them and for the leader. Slipstreaming leadership involves getting out front to lead the way for your teams, but also getting out of the way so they can do their part.

- Build teams that find a common purpose.
- Embrace selflessness.
- Discover diversity.
- Fill your gaps.
- Plant in fertile ground.

REFLECT

- What are some of your weaknesses that create gaps in your team? Is there someone else on the team who can fill those gaps, or should you consider hiring someone with the skills or passions that you lack?
- How can you promote teams that embrace diverse experiences, skills, and thinking?

PART II

Going Full Throttle

CHAPTER 5

Master the Maneuvers

Like many entrepreneurs, I began a company by focusing on things I loved to do and could do well. I've found that no matter where you are in an organization, combining those two vital ingredients—passion and expertise—produces high-octane fuel for success. If you love what you do and you're great at doing it, you'll move much faster down whatever road you're on. You will grow. Your team will grow. Your organization will grow. And growth is good, right?

Well, maybe it's good, but it's not always easy. In fact, for many of us, growth is often a series of crazy steep, downhill, 180-degree blind curves that have the potential to send us sliding headlong into a ditch. We may know that growth is "out there." We sense it; we want it. Then it comes upon us suddenly, and the realities of it are seldom exactly what we anticipated. It's hard to stay under control, and that's no fun when we're flying down the highway full throttle.

When your career and organization begin experiencing some momentum, however, there's a natural inclination to go faster, faster, faster. You don't want to miss the window of opportunity. This, I believe, is one of the most challenging phases in a leader's journey. It certainly has been for me.

This type of fast-paced growth can distract you from your destination, prevent you from enjoying the journey, or both. But by leading through the turn, you can see what's coming and organize your world accordingly—in real time. You don't lose focus on where you are, but you know the road is changing and you adjust. You master the maneuvers that allow you to successfully navigate rapid growth.

I learned a great deal about these maneuvers when I transitioned from a practitioner involved in every aspect of a start-up to a CEO building a rapidly growing, multimillion-dollar business that began operating on a national scale. I wish I could say I learned everything I needed all at once, implemented it, and immediately began reaping the benefits. But the reality is that I learned these maneuvers slowly over a period of years as we managed through the various stages of growth.

Growing Pains

Mitchell Communications Group began in 1995 as more of a consultancy than an agency, and it stayed that way for most of the first 10 years. The business largely revolved around me getting the work, doing the work, or assigning the work out to a small group of subcontractors. The company grew at a steady but modest pace.

Success, however, eventually resulted in growth spurts that were consistent with what's known as the Greiner Curve. Larry Greiner, professor emeritus of management and organization at the University of Southern California, came up with this model for organizational growth in 1972 and updated it, adding a sixth stage, in 1998. He points out that organizations grow until they reach a predictable crisis point. If they address the crisis successfully, they grow through the next stage until they hit the next predictable crisis point. Each crisis point requires different solutions, and each of the six phases requires different approaches from management and leadership. This was Mitchell Communications: Growth. Crisis point. Address it. Growth. Crisis point. Address it.

The first growth spurt began in 2005, which is what spurred me to hire Michael Clark. We had already been working with Walmart and J.B. Hunt, and that summer we won the national public relations account for Tyson Foods. I desperately needed a number two. Getting Michael was a coup because he was a talented competitor in Northwest Arkansas. I wooed him away from his brother's ad agency, which was based in Little Rock. Michael saw the opportunity to grow Mitchell into something substantial if we joined forces. To his credit, he was willing to take a big leap of faith and leave a secure situation, not to mention leaving his brother's company, to go with something quite unpredictable.

I'll never forget the day we fully committed to grow into something bigger than a consultancy. We had been driving hard for new business, and we were getting more and more work. But we were starting to feel the pressures of that success. The tipping point came at the end of a long week when Michael had been dealing extensively with a tough client situation. As we talked through it, his frustration mounted until he finally just stood up, said, "I have to go," and walked out the door.

What does that mean? I thought. *For good? Or will he be back tomorrow?*

He came back the next day, thankfully, and I told him I didn't want us to be miserable in our work. We could walk away from clients anytime we wanted. We could go back to being small, if that was more rewarding. I loved working with clients, and it gave me joy. But I could already foresee that the more we grew, the less time I would have with clients. So I was on the fence about our future.

"I don't want to get small," Michael said. "I want to build something really great."

At that point I knew I wanted that, too. Right then and there we committed to building a bigger company, and a great company. We started making plans, taking action, and making progress.

In the first year, we doubled the business. Over the next three years, we grew from about $750,000 annually in revenue to more than $2.5 million, and from 3 full-time employees to 13. As we developed an incredibly experienced leadership team, we were on the verge of making something substantial happen.

In early 2007, we moved into a quaint old house in a cool neighborhood right off the downtown square. It had a red front door and a wraparound front porch. Every time someone came in the side door, one of the neighbor's cats would slip in to visit. We often held our team meetings around the kitchen table, complete with a buffet of home-cooked food.

It was a fun time because we were thoroughly enjoying ourselves in that little house while the business was really growing. In fact, we outgrew it pretty quickly. As 2008 came to a close, we invested a significant amount of our profits into the company to help get it to the next level. We leased new office space, staffed up, migrated to a business enterprise software system, and acquired the training business I had cofounded eight years earlier with one of my best friends, Blake Woolsey. We'd placed all our bets on what looked like strong future growth.

Blake and I had founded the training business in 2000 in response to clients who were asking me for everything from media training to sales training. I lacked the capacity to deliver training, and I knew I needed to develop curriculum—I didn't want to just do anything off the shelf. Blake, one of the most talented speakers I know, agreed to partner with me to found Executive Communications Consultants (ECC), and it grew to include training, facilitation, and executive coaching.

We wrote dozens of original trainings and finally reached a point when we had to make a decision: put infrastructure and a support staff in place, or sell it to Mitchell and merge it into the agency, which had the staffing and resources we needed. So Mitchell acquired ECC in 2008, and Blake became the leader of the Center for Training, Business and Leadership Excellence— or the Center, as we refer to it today.

She was a significant leadership and talent acquisition for the agency, and we have benefited tremendously from her contributions. But when we acquired ECC and ramped up the other investments in our agency in 2008, we met one big hurdle to our growth that we hadn't anticipated: a recession.

Technically, the Great Recession began in December 2007, but recessions don't really have start and stop dates. They begin with a slow boil and are hard to recognize until they are out of control. For us, the reality of the recession hit as the leaves were changing in early fall of 2008. Lehman Brothers had filed for bankruptcy. Washington Mutual was heading into receivership. The subprime mortgage crisis was in full bloom. Suddenly our plans for growth looked like sunflowers facing a long, harsh winter.

It was September, and we had gathered as a team to celebrate our move to a new building.* We would have an entire floor, giving us room to spread out and grow. It should have been a festive evening. Despite my high hopes for a great night, however, I quickly realized my team wasn't worried about where they were going to sit in the new office. They were wondering whether they'd have a job by the end of the year.

You may have found yourself in a similar situation, either at that time or in other challenging times. The recession tested the mettle of everyone, not just entrepreneurs like me. As a leader, no matter how hard you try to be ready for anything, some unexpected challenge will happen and you won't know how to respond. This is especially true during growth spurts, because the business can change so quickly. When these situations arise, others turn to you for answers you just don't have. What do you do then?

That September night in 2008 was just such a situation for me. As I looked at the faces of my team, I knew I had to figure out our next move. So I simply dug deep and spoke to my passionate belief in our ability to succeed.

---

* I later learned our new building wasn't just any building; it was a historical landmark, originally built in 1905 and formerly a theater. When my parents visited after we first moved in, they told me the building was where they had gone on their first date in the 1950s to see a movie when they were students at the University of Arkansas. It had fallen into disrepair in the 1990s, so the mayor and city council planned to tear it down and, as the song goes, put up a parking lot. Instead, a 12-year-old boy collected enough signatures opposing that idea, so the city relented and the building was renovated.

I got everyone's attention, looked them all in the eyes and told them, "Do not be afraid of what you cannot control; instead focus all your energy on what you can control. I believe clients are dying to meet agency partners like us who are smart, results-oriented, hardworking, nimble, and determined. I believe not only will we survive; we'll thrive. I believe we are on the cusp of greatness."

At that point, the mood in the room changed. We began talking openly about what we were afraid of and what we could do to win in spite of what was swirling around us. This gave us confidence and a clear direction, and it became a turning point for the company.

The recession created a speed bump of sorts. But we rallied as a team and recommitted to growing our business even in the tough economic climate. We worked hard into the next year, determined to make this our reality. We were very fortunate that several of our longtime clients in industries such as retail, food, and energy actually were doing really well. As they succeeded, so did we—in fact, far more than we could have predicted. During the next two years, growth came over us like a waterfall. We found ourselves with more work than we'd ever had before, and more was on the way.

During 2009 and 2010, we grew revenue from $2 million to $6.5 million. We grew full-time staff from 13 to 37, including our future president, Sarah Clark. Sarah had been a client for nine years before leaving Walmart to spend more time with her son, Eli, whom she had adopted from Siberia. Once Eli had acclimated to his new home and Sarah was ready to return to the workforce, she agreed to join us as a senior vice president, instead of taking any of the other offers she had. Sarah headed our corporate communications division, a position I created to get someone of her caliber and expertise.

This time period also was a turning point for the agency because we started our creative department. Most small-to-midsize agencies hadn't ventured into the creative services arena, but we were able to get ahead of the competition by hiring a creative leader from the ad industry, who was a game changer for Mitchell. It allowed us to diversify our revenue and move into content creation ahead of our competitors. We began offering creative services such as copywriting, graphic design, website design and development, social media platform design and content creation, social media training and consulting, digital asset management, and e-communications.

At the same time, we were moving into video and digital production. Our first hire was a young, talented graduate of John Brown University with a degree in digital cinema production, photography, and broadcasting. We had hired him and another producer on several occasions to handle our growing video work, so it was a natural next step for us to begin building this capability in-house, and we were fortunate to get him. In a way, we were leading through the turn by offering services before they were popular at other agencies.

To accommodate our growth, we took over the remaining three floors of our four-story building; our office space grew from 4,400 square feet to nearly 12,000 square feet. During 2011, we grew to 61 employees and $11.5 million in revenues. We launched another new practice area (digital and social), and we acquired two major new clients: Hilton Hotels & Resorts and Procter & Gamble. In fact, we experienced 445 percent growth over a four-year period from 2008 to 2011.

During all of that time, however, one question lingered. It was the same question we faced the day we agreed there was no turning back from growth: How do we grow bigger, stay great as a company, and find joy in our work?

You see, growth wasn't the problem. We had the passion and expertise to succeed and an abundance of opportunity. Managing and adapting to the rapid growth was the problem. Our once small company that ran on organized chaos quickly had become a growing company that was less organized and more chaotic. We had to lead and operate differently, but we weren't sure how.

As a leader, I had to master the maneuvers of rapid growth or that growth could kill our company, make us all miserable, or both. Here are the maneuvers I've learned that helped us navigate the stages of rapid growth.

Maneuver No. 1: Admit You Don't Know. Then Go Find the Answers.

Success brought us face-to-face with the types of challenges all rapidly growing companies have. Maybe you've been someplace like this and can relate to challenges such as:

- Not having enough staff
- Not having enough time to interview job candidates
- Once they're hired, not having enough time to train them

And not just people challenges. Rapidly growing companies have plenty of operational challenges, too, such as:

- Processes and systems created for a smaller company that now strain to handle a much greater volume of work
- Not enough technology—both hardware and software

- Not enough office space
- Worst of all, a leadership team working overtime and then some trying to keep all the balls in the air—with stress beginning to take a toll

I found myself running from one thing to the next, sticking my finger in the dike everywhere I could. But it was clear to me something bigger had to be done to manage this flood of growth before we all drowned. The problem was, I had no idea what to do. I'd never been *here* before—facing a challenge of this magnitude. Everyone was looking to me for the answers.

I also found myself at a leadership crossroads. I needed to pick the right path—right now—for our firm or risk watching it all fall apart.

Have you ever felt this way: that the challenge before you as a leader was so great that you might not be able to lead effectively through it? One of the worst feelings a leader can have is self-doubt. That's a dark place to be. But if you can identify why you doubt yourself and change that, you can take the first step down a new path.

My self-doubt was based on one simple thing: lack of knowledge about what to do in this specific situation. It was compounded by the fact that I knew few people to turn to, as not many companies were growing during the recession. Fortunately, I recognized two things:

- I knew there were things I didn't know.
- I needed to do whatever it took to find those things out.

I first began addressing this challenge in the fall of 2009, when I set out for Hanover, New Hampshire, for a week of executive education at the Tuck School of Business at Dartmouth. I'd always wanted to do an executive education class, and now was the time. I attended "Growing the Minority Business to Scale" and spent five days—and most nights—totally immersed in the learning process, trying to figure out everything I could from our professors and my classmates, who were also entrepreneurs, and then applying it to our situation at Mitchell.

As a result of what I learned at Tuck, I worked with our leadership team to develop a plan to strengthen our business and address our most pressing needs by focusing on four things:

1. Operations
2. Growth
3. People
4. Culture

Underpinning this plan was a focus on further developing our legal savvy, as well as more sophisticated financial controls to help us sustain our growth for the long run.

Over the course of the next few years:

- we made a lot of **big** decisions as a company
- we took some calculated risks to invest in talent, technology, and infrastructure
- I spent a great deal of my time simply being a storyteller—sharing the history of our company, talking about our values, and creating ways to bring our unique and compelling culture to life—and not just for our current employees, but for the new people we were bringing in, as well

I also endured more than a few sleepless nights wondering if any of this was going to work.

I knew I didn't have all the answers to our growth challenges. I was an expert in public relations, not a classically trained business management professional. Not knowing, however, was only a problem if I couldn't admit that I needed help and if I didn't find the help I needed.

That's why attending the growth program at Dartmouth, and a leadership program a few years later at Harvard, proved so valuable. And that's why having mentors, surrounding myself with talented leaders and consultants, and turning over every possible stone of information and wisdom I could find has proven so valuable.

When you're growing as a leader, by definition you're finding yourself on unmarked highways. You can ask for directions or wander aimlessly. My advice: do whatever it takes to find the right path.

Maneuver No. 2: Upgrade your ride.

When I started Mitchell Communications, I was the quarterback for the team—and the running back . . . the wide receiver . . . the entire offensive line . . . the coach . . . and the water girl. You get the idea. I did it all. When I hired people to help, they did it all, too. We all did it all.

I remember the days when I would go to a client meeting, take notes on the client's needs, come back and figure out how we could tackle those needs, and then write a proposal with deliverables, pricing, and a plan. When we secured the contract, I would figure out how we would implement the plan. I found excitement and fulfillment in being able to do it all, in becoming essentially a master craftsman.

If I needed help, whoever was available would help. If someone else needed help with a project, I'd jump in and lend a hand. That's the way it is when you have a small team. It's like tossing balls. Something's going on, and somebody tosses you the ball. You catch it, and you run with it. Work gets done in a spontaneous manner that's based more on the availability of people to jump in and help than on organized structure, roles, and responsibilities.

Then there comes a day when you realize you can't always catch the ball and run with it. It no longer works for you and your team to catch-as-catch-can. As the leader, you need a game plan, which means you have to spend more time coaching the team or planning and managing the game. You need to step out of the practitioner's role and into more of a strategist's role where you're not doing everything from start to finish.

To do this, you need more structure. One of the key lessons I learned at Dartmouth was that operations, processes, and systems become critical pieces that allow an organization to successfully maneuver—and make the most of—growth. When these are done well, it keeps you and your organization heading in the right direction and allows you the freedom to enjoy the experience.

I first realized the need for more structure in my company in 2011. I always had an open organization, so everybody was in the leadership group and involved in all the decision making. But in about two years we had tripled in size to nearly 45 full-time employees, and it was time to put in a new layer of leadership—an executive committee. It consisted of five senior-level leaders who represented the different parts of the organization.

Instead of collaborating with 15 or 20 people in a leadership group about decisions, I could do that with just 5 people on the executive committee. This is a structure you might consider not only when your organization is growing, but when you find yourself with too many direct reports, or you simply need to concentrate your time with fewer leaders in order to make a bigger impact.

Frankly, I was scared to add another layer because I was afraid the organization would become hierarchical and that people would feel removed from me and the rest of the top leadership. It worked, however, because we kept the larger leadership group in place. We just met less frequently and I didn't bring every single thing to them. I still kept them very informed and sought their opinions at times, but the executive committee handled the more strategic decisions and the more confidential decisions such as finance and human resources.

We also created several ways of cascading communications through the organization so that everybody would feel connected and informed. As an organization grows and needs different levels of leadership, it's critical to have a process for communicating often and as transparently as possible so people don't feel like they're no longer in the know.

It's a culture-killer when people begin thinking, "We've become so big now that nobody cares anymore about me, and nobody communicates anymore with me." So we had a very intentional, specific plan for sharing information people wanted or needed to know so they never had to worry or wonder what was going on with the company. That's one of the ways you can overcome getting big and creating layers. You have to be very intentional and forthcoming about communication.

What that looks like, of course, can vary from one organization to the next, and technology is always changing the game. At Mitchell, we use video messages, all-office email, team meetings, departmental meetings, and staff meetings. Sometimes team leaders are expected to share information. We now have Kudos, a socialized employee recognition platform that works on the company intranet. You can post communication that every employee has access to and can read. Sometimes it's just walking the halls, talking to people, and checking in. "Hey, did you guys hear about this? What kind of questions do you have? Let me know if you want more information."

This structure is important because it allows you to accomplish the next, and perhaps most difficult, maneuver.

Maneuver No. 3: Release Your Leaders.

The idea of delegation goes back forever.

As communities formed, tasks were delegated based on skills and experiences that would best help the group: some hunted, some gathered, and some drew stick figures on the walls in caves. As cultures evolved into villages, cities, kingdoms, and empires, the delegation evolved with it. Not only did people gravitate toward certain roles, but they found that delegation provided a way to train new leaders (and other workers) for the roles that were essential for survival.

As old and proven as this solution is, however, delegation is still something leaders struggle with, especially during times of growth. This is when you as a craftsman have to challenge yourself to grow into the role of a real leader: someone who can let go and empower and equip others around you.

People who really like to be in control and who are really good at what they do often struggle to hand things off to others. When they do, they face the temptation to jump back in and take over at the first sign of trouble: "I can do it smarter," "I can do it faster," "I can certainly do it better than this team, because I'm the master craftsman," "I'm the one who designed this program or built the relationship with this client or developed this process."

But when you turn roles and responsibilities over to other people, you have to give them the good stuff that goes with it. You have to release them to lead. You can't give somebody a responsibility but then take the credit for what happens when that person does the job. Or you can't give someone a client relationship but still hold onto it so the client continues to call you.

You have to empower, equip, and enable people to succeed with what you're giving them. You have to knock all the barriers out of the way for them to become the star in the areas of responsibilities that you've given to them. You have to let go of the work but still stay close enough to coach them when they need help and make sure they're moving in the right direction.

When I committed to empowering others, I began to learn how beneficial it was to me, the people around me, and our organization. Other leaders would take things I use to do to a whole new level of excellence simply because they had a talent or an ability or a perspective that I lacked. They just gave the challenges more attention. When I took nine different things I was juggling and divided them among two or three different people, those capabilities in the organization became much better because those people had time to really dig in and do them well.

On the other hand, if you don't truly release leaders—that is, if you don't empower, equip, and enable them—you'll discover that the talented, capable, smart people you worked so hard to get on your team will soon leave for some other team. They should, because you aren't providing opportunities for them to reach their destinations and enjoy their journeys. Why would anyone stay with somebody who's selfish, driven by power, and hungry for credit?

That's not the leader I wanted to be. I wanted to help people around me grow. I wanted to watch them soar. When you do that as a leader, you keep great people on your team and you engender loyalty, confidence, and commitment from them. They'll walk through fire for you because you're helping them grow and shine, too. Not coincidentally, that's when your organization not only grows and shines, but soars.

Mastering these types of maneuvers as a leader will help you thrive in growth periods: not only big ones like we faced at Mitchell Communications, but also the more subtle ones. These maneuvers allow you to lead through the turn and make the adjustments to get you where you want to go.

The Road Ahead

REVIEW

The demands of rapid growth can drive a leader off course or cause you to lose your passion for your work, unless you learn ways to master the maneuvers to manage that growth by leading through the turn.

- Maneuver No. 1: Admit you don't know. Then go find the answers.
- Maneuver No. 2: Upgrade your ride.
- Maneuver No. 3: Release your leaders.

REFLECT

- Where do you see the most growth happening or likely to happen in your work? Is it personal growth? Team growth? Organizational growth?
- What processes are you and your teams using that are outdated and slowing you down?
- How well would your team rate you when it comes to releasing them to grow as leaders?

CHAPTER 6

Defining a Destiny

Not long ago we hired someone to work in our New York office, and I experienced one of those affirming moments all leaders cherish.

"I've had lots of opportunities," she told me, "but I picked Mitchell because I want to be in this kind of culture. I'm very impressed with your culture. Everybody talked about it. Everybody was consistent, all the way to the top. That's where I want to be—in that kind of environment."

One of the biggest challenges I've faced as a leader has been building and maintaining a culture that prompts people to say things like this new teammate said, and not just on their first day on the job, but for years to come. It's a challenge because a culture needs constant nurturing. You don't put it together like a jigsaw puzzle and then sit back and admire the picture. The very word *culture* originates from Latin, where it was all about agriculture: the cultivation of plants and fields. It's something that thrives and sustains when you commit to caring for it over time.

So in that sense, a culture has no destination. You never get there. But ironically, you can't create a great culture if you don't know where you're going. You have to define a destiny that inspires people to join you. That definition must include the *how* as well as the *where*. Because how you bring your destiny to life *is* your culture, and it determines whether you get where you're going and who will join you for the journey.

Culture, in fact, is a clear example of how critical the intersection of destination leadership and a journey mindset can be. Creating an environment where goals can be achieved by people who feel inspired and valued is the holy grail of leadership. Both where you're going and how you'll get there matter. When you have both, great things can happen, even when all odds are against you—especially when all the odds are against you.

A Formula for Culture

When discussions these days turn to organizations with great cultures, most people think of high-tech companies or other trendy start-ups that shower their employees with great pay and perks such as onsite game rooms or yoga classes: Google, Zappos, Warby Parker, Facebook.

I think of an energy company. In fact, one of the first things I learned from Southwestern Energy was the importance of defining a destiny when it comes to building a great culture. Programs and perks don't matter much if they don't align with the destiny, and for Southwestern Energy that destiny was defined with a formula that emerged during the darkest hours of its history.

"We had lost a major lawsuit over royalty payments in October of 1998, and we lost the appeal in June of 2000," Harold Korell, retired CEO of Southwestern Energy Company recalled. "We didn't have any cash to do anything with, and no one in the world wanted to talk to us. I was worried someone was just going to take us over because our stock price was also depressed at the time."

Harold had just joined the company in 1997, and he quickly found himself with a nearly insurmountable leadership challenge. The small company had lost nearly half of its value overnight due to the court's unfavorable decision.

In fact, the company's assets were worth more than its stock.

"We had a meeting to plan our annual report and its primary message," Harold said. "What do you say at a time like that? 'Let's just sell the assets and all go home?' We talked intently as a team for quite a while and agreed we had done a lot of the hard work already by putting the right people into place. We believed we had some really good projects that could create real value for the company."

As the meeting wore on, Harold went to a marker board and wrote what looked like a mathematical formula:

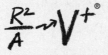

$$\frac{R^2}{A} \rightsquigarrow V^{+®}$$

He was trying to capture the essence of what the team believed: it had the right people doing the right things, and supported by the underlying assets of the company, the team could create exponential value—or value plus.

After some discussion about the inevitable ups and downs of pursuing value creation, Harold erased the equals sign and replaced it with an arrow that mirrors the challenging path to success, creating what has become known at Southwestern Energy as the "Formula."

"That became the theme for our annual report that year," said Harold. "I could say to a shareholder, 'You may not believe in us, but this is why *we* believe in us. If we have the right people doing the right things and assets that are creating cash, and if we invest that right, then we'll create more value. Therefore, we have a reason to exist. It's one thing to think about selling the company and its assets today, but you might be better off if you stay with us and allow us to create more value for you.'"

Instead of giving up, Harold and his team defined a vision for where it wanted to go and how it would rebuild. They made some bold decisions to jump-start the business and began sharing their story with shareholders, investors, and employees.

"We were right," said Harold.

Over the next decade, Southwestern Energy became the number one performing stock in the S&P 500, increasing 5,776 percent from January 1, 2000, through December 31, 2009, outpacing even Apple. The company has continued to grow at a strong pace, and today it is the third-largest producer of natural gas in the US Lower 48. Even as commodity prices have fallen and times have grown hard on energy companies, its mission is still driven by the Formula: to create value+ by providing energy to the world. The Formula represents the essence of the company's corporate philosophy and how it operates.

Southwestern Energy has been a client of Mitchell Communications since the early 2000s, and we've been fortunate to work with them as they experienced dramatic growth and success. Harold and I have talked on many occasions about the company's compelling culture, how it came to be, and how critical it was as Southwestern Energy experienced rapid growth.

"While there were so many things involved in our success, it really comes down to the Formula," said Harold, who retired as CEO in 2009 and as chairman of the board in 2014. "We had the right people—people who had curiosity, who were innovative, creative, hardworking, who know right from wrong. They began to interpret the Formula to mean things that were empowering to them, saying, 'I must be one of the right people.' And feeling good about yourself is part of doing good."

Indeed the beliefs represented by the Formula are timeless. If you ask the company's current CEO, Bill Way, what the Formula means to the company today, he shares thoughts quite similar to Harold's—but expressed in a different way.

"It's very much a source of inspiration and guidance for all of us," said Bill. "The Formula and our core values form the foundation of our culture and our strategy. During the recent collapse in product prices, we took a visible leadership role in halting drilling and completions operations. While an extremely difficult decision, impacting hundreds of people, our Formula speaks of 'the right people doing the right things, wisely investing the cash flow from our underlying assets.' The Formula anchors our decisions and how we act, when prices are high and when they are not."

Bill told me he was especially proud of how quickly the team rallied around cost and margin improvement, enabling them to return the company to strength and resume investment. "One thing is for sure, we never lost focus on our corporate responsibility work, which includes assuring safe and healthy workplaces for our employees as well as a commitment to environmental stewardship, philanthropy and community engagement."

Bill sums it up best. "Our Formula is enduring. The culture that has been built upon its wise principles enables us to thrive in good times and bad and deliver value+ to all of our stakeholders. It represents the true spirit of Southwestern Energy."

The Formula was created during one of the company's darkest times. But, it became the foundation upon which the company's compelling culture was built and brought to life during the good times and bad that followed—and will for many years to come.

Building Mitchell's Culture

I learned a lot about the importance of culture by working closely with Harold. It was during this time that I began to crystallize my own thinking about establishing a compelling approach to our work, a common team spirit, a collaborative nature, and a collegial environment.

As we started experiencing dramatic growth, I knew I wanted to continue some of the things that had worked so well with LocalLink and add new things that better suited an expanding full-time team. So over the second decade of Mitchell's history, 2005 to 2015, we established five signature culture programs, we made conscious decisions about how to invest in our people, and we worked hard to become an employer of choice.

But the agency needed something more powerful than a collection of programs if we were to have a truly compelling and sustainable culture. The Formula became a destiny definer for

Southwestern Energy, and we needed a similarly clear foundation for how we would do things. Programs come and go. We needed something durable. And just like Southwestern Energy, when we needed it most, we found it.

Things came to a head in the summer of 2009. We faced a rising tide of new work and an increasing need for more team members, but everyone was too busy to interview prospective employees. Even if we could hire someone, no one had time to train them. So we were spiraling further into a black hole.

Finally, COO Michael Clark and I decided to bring in several candidates for our leadership team to interview in one jam-packed day. It was a good idea in many ways and it helped us make some key hires, but it also exacerbated a problem that had been brewing. By the end of the day, our leaders were mentally exhausted and several faced an all-nighter to catch up on the work they had put off to focus on finding new team members. Their frustration with the situation seeped out to the group. Some harsh words were exchanged and plenty of voices were raised, until I found myself jumping in the middle of things to keep the peace.

That evening as I was leaving the office, one of our leaders told me pretty bluntly: "You're the only one who wants to grow, Elise. The rest of us are just worn out."

That comment crushed and disappointed me, until I realized it was only partly true. The team really did want to be part of a growing company; they just didn't like the personal toll it was taking on them. This was exactly what I was trying to fix, but I could see that simply adding more head count wasn't going to solve the whole problem. We needed to address something deeper.

After a sleepless night or two, I decided one thing we were missing was shared team norms. These are the principles by which a team agrees to treat one another. Blake Woolsey and I had helped many teams write their norms when we were conducting workshops through our other company, Executive Communications Consultants (now known as the Center). So I was well aware of this concept and knew we needed it.

When I called our team together for an unscheduled meeting, the look on their faces told me what they were thinking: "Why is she taking more of our time again when we just spent an entire day not getting any client work done?" But I knew the time we were getting ready to spend together could change everything.

"We're going to fix some underlying issues," I told them. "Today we need to agree as a group how we're going to work together more effectively, and more specifically how we want to treat each other. Let's start by brainstorming: what does this group absolutely need to have in place to function at its best?"

After a few minutes of silence, someone finally spoke up: "Trust. We need to trust each other more, to be reliable and to do what we say we'll do so no one has to go around checking behind others to make sure something got done on time and at the right quality level."

A great start. And from there the list grew until it became obvious that we were defining our values as a group. Each of us had individual values, but we'd never established a common set of values: a "true north" to guide us as we grew together.

Once we had the list, we decided our next best step was to take it to the larger team. We didn't want to choose our company values for everyone; we wanted it to be an employee-led process. So we shortened the list to the five things we felt the strongest about. We held an all-employee working lunch, where small groups took one of the five words and fleshed out what it looked like when we were truly living the spirit of that word. Each group also had the power to change the word if they thought of something better.

We ended up with the original words still on the list, but with fantastic thinking about how we would live out these ideals on an everyday basis. What we came up with still stands as our values:

Trust

- Honest, transparent, forthcoming
- Reliable, dependable: we do what we say we'll do
- Treating others as you would like to be treated

Open Communication

- Encouraging healthy debate to bring our best thinking forward
- Challenging underlying assumptions
- Ensuring clear understanding
- Resolving conflict productively
- Appreciating the professional knowledge, skills, and contributions of others

Service

- Anticipating the needs of others
- Being responsive
- Offering strategic counsel

Results

- Goal-oriented
- Delivering results that are valued and recognized by others
- Ensuring excellence, quality

- Being dedicated, demonstrating drive and a strong work ethic
- Recognizing contribution

Commitment
- To integrity
- To our clients
- To our profession
- To each other

To clarify, our values are aspirational, as all values should be. I'm the first to admit we're not perfect. But we get up every day trying to live up to them, and I think knowing what's expected of everyone means a lot to our team members.

They are a powerful reminder of how we want to live and work every day. They guide the decisions we make and the actions we take. They allow us to hold each other accountable for how we behave. They give us a foundation for dealing with organizational change, like mergers and acquisitions or opening new offices in different cities. They guide our hiring. And they shape how we deal with what I call "cultural scoundrels": people who can be high performers but who don't live up to our values and cultural norms, and end up creating more havoc than they're worth. We work with these people to help them improve their behaviors, but sometimes it's best for us—and them—for them to leave.

In short, we've learned the powerful combination of weaving our business goals and company values together to make sure we're focused on not only *what's* being accomplished, but also *how* it's being accomplished. Values should enable employees to make decisions that not only propel the company forward but also ensure the company is a place where people want to work.

More Than Words

Once we had our values in place, coming up with ways to bring them to life became nearly second nature to us and something I thought about frequently. I wanted them to be more than words on paper, so we needed tangible initiatives to show how Mitchell was different.

One of the ways we did this was by taking a more dedicated approach to human resources. In the early days of Mitchell, Marla and I had handled this pretty well. But in the fall of 2011, we were growing so dramatically that I walked into Michael's office one day and announced, "I quit."

As the blood drained from his face, I realized I hadn't made myself very clear, so I added, ". . . as HR director. I don't think I can do it anymore." There were just too many things I didn't know, and I was afraid I'd make a mistake out of ignorance that could become a legal issue for us.

We were fortunate to recruit a top-notch human resources professional who brought tremendous knowledge and capability to the agency. I've found that a strong human resources department helped us create the structures and implement programs that bring our values to life and ensure we maintain the culture we've worked so hard to build.

There are many ways you can bring your values to life, but I want to share six that have worked well over time for Mitchell. The first is about pay and benefits, but I also believe your culture should shine in unique ways that reflect your values and underscore your organization's business strategy. So the rest revolve around the five signature programs that give us greater opportunities to demonstrate our commitment to our employees, our industry, and our community.

1. Share the Wealth

One of the most important parts of an employee-employer relationship is compensation. As our full-time ranks began to swell, I recognized the need to be competitive, not just in pay but with an entire compensation package.

As hard as it was to find qualified talent to hire in Northwest Arkansas, I didn't want to lose employees over a small increase in base salary they might find somewhere else. We already offered professional development dollars, companywide outings, and other nice perks, but we began adding new benefits that I thought would make a difference.

First, we decided to offer 100 percent employer-paid health care benefits to all full-time employees. This was pretty unheard of, but we found a way to make it work, and it made us extremely competitive—in many cases, a far more attractive employer.

We also wanted to share wealth with our team. So we established an informal practice of giving a year-end bonus to every employee no matter what they did or how long they had been employed. In fact, one year a graphic designer lucked out on his timing; his first day was the day we were distributing bonuses, so we included him in the process and gave him one, too.

We used this time to reinforce our company's culture and illustrate how important every member of the team was to our success. We brought small groups to my office, and Michael and I spent about 30 minutes sharing stories about the company's year and highlighting ways in which they had contributed to our growth and progress. Then I would hand each person an envelope with a bonus check.

This was always one of my favorite days of the year, and I think it was pretty popular with our employees, too. It got me thinking about how I could do even more for our key leaders. So we worked with our legal advisors to devise more formal ways of wealth-sharing. Among other things, we created a bonus initiative called KEEP—Key Employee Excellence Program— that rewarded directors and above with an annual bonus based on the company's performance. It included a vesting period to encourage retention.

While people care about money, of course, and the benefits they receive, sharing wealth isn't just about giving people more compensation. It's also about showing your people that you care for them and appreciate what they do. I always knew we would never have been as successful as we were without a highly accomplished and productive team. I wanted them to see we believed in their ability to deliver for clients and their do-whatever-it-takes attitude, and that when we achieved success as a team, their individual efforts would be rewarded, too. In this way, we demonstrated our values of trust, results, and commitment.

2. Promote Diversity: Big Break

Fostering diversity and inclusion is a core competency at Mitchell. We believe a more diverse and inclusive workplace makes us stronger as a company and helps us serve our clients' needs to reach increasingly diverse audiences. Diverse thinking and incorporating broad points of view in ideation and decision making almost always yields a better result.

Living this out isn't always easy when you're based in Northwest Arkansas. In 2000, the metro area had about 350,000 people and only 14 percent were from ethnically diverse backgrounds. By 2012, the population had grown to nearly half a million. The Caucasian population had grown by 18.5 percent. Other groups had grown much faster: Hispanic Americans by 139.3 percent, African Americans by 113.8 percent, Asian Americans (or Pacific Islanders) by 207.1 percent. These groups still represented less than 25 percent of the population.[1] So it is now, and historically has been, a challenge for companies in the region to find and hire top talent from minority backgrounds. As a small company, we definitely faced this issue, and it's also a challenge throughout the public relations industry, particularly in agencies.

To help us attract more diverse talent, we developed "Big Break," an all-expenses-paid, weeklong internship during spring break for high-performing graduating college seniors. Big Break gives students real-world experience while working with talented peers from across the country. It's also an opportunity for Mitchell to introduce potential job candidates from diverse backgrounds to our agency, while showcasing a community and region they may not have previously considered.

Each year we accept nominations from students at top-notch communications programs, including several minority-serving institutions. The 6 to 10 students we select are immersed in the world of agency life. They have one-on-one visits with our leaders and receive customized trainings to provide insight about working in the industry. In some years they have worked in teams with selected nonprofit organizations on specific communications challenges. During the first year alone, we offered jobs to five participants, with four accepting.

Big Break became well-known among our clients, but it is just one way we are proactive and creative in tackling our diversity challenges. For instance, we've also formed task forces and brought together representatives from clients for discussions and to look for ways to promote regional diversity and inclusion.

As a result, we've made several key hires and continue to broaden our multicultural capabilities to help clients build relationships with diverse stakeholder groups. We've also reinforced our values of trust and open communication.

3. Celebrate Accomplishments: Bright Spots

In our early days, we often used the excuse that we were just "too busy" to mark our milestones. But research shows that celebrating small wins can be critical to long-term success and employee happiness.[2] In the life of an entrepreneur, risks and setbacks are so common that celebrating small markers of success can boost morale and refuel you for the fight ahead. Having a journey mindset means you can take some time to stop, look around, and appreciate the beauty of where you are, no matter what might happen tomorrow.

To help us do this, we established Bright Spots meetings to shine the light on our employees and their performance on behalf of clients. Teams present a project they've been working on, any learnings they discovered, and opportunities they found for cross-team collaboration. We also use these times to highlight company values, employee promotions, and client relationships. In addition to Bright Spots, we hold cookouts, tailgates, and ice-cream parties; bring food trucks on-site; and hold other informal celebrations to honor team accomplishments.

We've found it's important to be mindful and intentional in how we praise our team. Recognition is a powerful motivator, and what leaders praise is noticed by everyone. We try to spotlight the behaviors we want to encourage. Performance is at the top of the list, of course. But if praise is solely performance-based, you'll breed a performance culture. It will no longer matter how employees achieve results as long as they're achieving them. This kind of focus can diminish the meaning and impact of your values, which will hurt your company's ability to succeed long-term.

We often recognize team members who exhibit one or more of our values in their actions, and we have in recent years implemented an online recognition program. This allows all team members to post thanks or recognition on a fellow employee's page and the agency's wall. Team members can also give a badge to someone for a value that the person has demonstrated in his or her work.

Celebrating small wins and publicly appreciating hard work helps us live out our values of open communication and results. It yields better morale, a greater sense of meaning, and subsequently, a higher level of employee retention. Year after year, our employee survey reflects how much our team appreciates these things. Our annual turn-over rate at the agency is often in the low teens, half of the industry average.

4. Develop Your Leaders: Accelerate

We all recognize the importance of a talented team, but we should not fool ourselves into believing we will always keep our best employees. Competitors will attempt to woo them away as we become more successful. One way to combat this is to invest in your people with a variety of benefits—not all related to money.

We help our employees grow through professional development trainings offered through the Center (our training division). One of my favorite trainings is Accelerate, an emerging leaders program designed to give high-potential employees a chance to flex their leadership muscle and develop new skills as they grow their responsibilities in the firm.

Accelerate helped us tackle a potential problem. We had a number of talented young professionals who were eager to rise in the ranks but lacked the knowledge and experience to jump head-first into significant leadership roles. These young guns are the ones you're most in danger of losing. Accelerate became a way to give them training and hands-on opportunities to grow as new leaders, setting them up for success when an opening came up.

Throughout the six-month course, which is designed and taught by the Center, they are given the opportunity for deep-dive learning, teamwork, stretch assignments, creativity, and innovation. They're also given an opportunity to present their recommendations on a business challenge. Graduation is a special occasion, taking place at a Bright Spots meeting with all employees present. Each graduate is recognized for their accomplishments in the program and given an original piece of art created by a local sculpture that bears the Accelerate logo and the agency's values.

Since it kicked off in 2012, Accelerate has allowed us to equip more than 25 rising leaders at the agency, and more than

90 percent received promotions during or after graduating from the program. It's also been a key way we've lived out the values of service, results, and commitment.

5. Encourage Giving: Ignite

One of the most powerful ways to motivate a workforce is by enabling them to help others. Our Ignite program gives money and time off to teams of employees to do random acts of kindness in our community.[3] It was inspired by a giving experience that changed my life and allowed me to expand upon my wealth-sharing philosophy. (I'll share this story in more detail in Chapter 13.)

Ignite kicks off each January with a day of giving and lives throughout the year as employees receive time off to volunteer in the communities where we have offices. Since it began in 2010, we've made cash and in-kind donations to help dozens of local nonprofits and individuals in need, ranging from homeless shelters, veterans service programs, elementary schools, organizations working with abused and neglected children, and victims of domestic violence. In 2016, the entire agency focused on supporting organizations that champion women and serve women's needs as a way to underscore our heritage as a women-owned and led company.

It has been a powerful program for us and given us a far greater return than we could have imagined: employees develop deeper relationships by sharing the giving experience with each other; they see a greater connection between company values and their own; and they grow as individuals through understanding challenges that are facing their community in a real and immediate way.

Ignite represents our values of trust, service, and commitment. It provides a priceless experience for our employees, and most important, an invaluable opportunity to see how blessed we have been and how important it is that we continue to bless those around us.

6. Create Ambassadors: Keepers of the Seal

Inviting our employees to become brand ambassadors is another way we bring our values to life. For instance, we regularly gather new employees for a breakfast. More than muffins and chitchat, it gives me the chance to tell our brand's story. I take them through a brief presentation, narrating each era of the company's history: significant turning points, how we reacted, what we learned, and how our decisions propelled us forward. Then I invite each of them to become a Keeper of the Seal.

The Keeper of the Seal is a tradition that began in the time of Edward the Confessor, who ruled England from 1042 to 1066. The seal symbolized the integrity of the country, and its keeper was a figure of great esteem, designated the most trustworthy and honorable of all the king's subjects.

The seal represents trust in our company, too. When we invite employees to become Keepers of the Seal, we're asking them to become guardians of the Mitchell brand—to feel a sense of ownership and pride in the company. This time together also allows me to be a storyteller, recounting our vibrant history and bringing our compelling culture to life in our employees' minds.

Creating this sense of ownership is a way to live out our values of trust, open communication, and commitment. It's one of the key ways we create cultural champions, team members who live the culture.

Top Down

Culture starts at the top. No matter the size of your team or the stage of growth you're in, you, as a leader, set the tone for how business gets done and what it's like to work in your organization. You define the destiny: the where and the how. You are the CCO—the chief culture officer. But it can't begin and end with you.

Especially as your team grows, it becomes harder to find time for those meaningful lunches and small group conversations. So while you never give up the CCO title, your role changes. You need more cultural champions because a great culture doesn't hinge on a single leader, or even a leadership team. It must live throughout the entire organization, happening organically between people and in the regular interactions they have with each other. When this happens, your culture can actually drive your organization's success.

For Mitchell, we have long described ourselves as a "high performance, high values" company, meaning that both are necessary for our success. If we live up to both, we attract the right kind of people who want to work with us. Talented people want to work with other talented people and great customers, and "excellence attracts excellence" is a self-perpetuating philosophy that yields powerful overall results.

Over time, I have realized the power of a compelling culture, one built on values and brought to life through unique and engaging initiatives like Ignite and Big Break. I often hear our employees refer to their "Mitchell family" and how much their teammates mean to them. I am well aware that many receive job offers from other employers, yet our turn-over rate is half the industry average, which is a good indicator of the cultural health of the company.

Employees who, through countless emails and conversations, want to tell me what they appreciate about the agency is another indicator of the cultural health of the company. For example, last Thanksgiving, one of our content strategists, who has had at least two other offers, wrote me to say: "Thank you for giving me the opportunity to make Mitchell a part of my life every day. I'll forever be thankful for that." Another rising star on our client service team wrote to say: "I wanted to reach out with a huge thank you for allowing me to be a part of the Mitchell family for the last few years. There are so many things I've always loved about Mitchell—too many to mention. I'm truly appreciative of all the knowledge, opportunities, and friendships that simply wouldn't be mine if I hadn't come to Mitchell." Another on our new business team shared with me recently: "It has been an amazing experience to work with you and this wonderful team. Not only do we care about the work we do, the company and clients we do it for but it is the great people we work with that makes the task that much more rewarding. . . . There are many companies that talk about nurturing an environment for development and progression but Mitchell encourages and motivates the staff to be the best they can be."

Clearly our culture is powerful, and the signature programs only help make our culture tangible and an obvious difference-maker in the war for talent. The culture they help create underscores the importance of thinking not just about the destination, or how we grow in terms of size and profits, but also about the journey and that *how* we go about getting there matters just as much.

The Road Ahead

REVIEW

It is possible and essential to merge destination leadership and a journey mindset when growing a successful culture in any organization. That's because a culture needs a shared destination and a shared approach for getting there. Defining a destiny involves both the *how* and the *where*, and it helps shape the culture for long-term success. Here are the ways in which we brought culture to life at Mitchell:

1. Share the wealth.
2. Promote diversity.
3. Celebrate accomplishments.
4. Develop your leaders.
5. Encourage giving.
6. Create ambassadors.

REFLECT

- Do you have company values that resonate with you and your team, and are they more than words on paper? What are ways you could help bring those values to life more frequently?
- How well is your culture seen and felt in the regular interactions your team has with each other? Do you have an opportunity to empower other culture champions to ensure culture lives beyond you?

CHAPTER 7

Steer Left. Turn Right.

I remember the day my colleagues at work *all* came to see me. One by one, they had learned I was taking up motorcycling, and finally they decided they needed to do an intervention of sorts. As a group they walked in to figure out what in the world I was up to and hopefully, talk me out of it.

"Do you know how dangerous that is?"

"Are you wearing a helmet?"

"You're taking a safety course, aren't you?"

And then someone voiced what was on all of their minds:

"What if something happens to you? What will happen to us?"

And all along I'd been thinking they were concerned about me.

"Well, that, too," they said.

I got it, of course. They loved me and cared about me. They didn't want anything bad to happen to me. But they didn't really understand my drive to ride. They're not the first ones.

Melissa Holbrook Pierson, a passionate biker and author of *The Perfect Vehicle*, believes you can divide the world into two

127

groups: "Those who do, those who don't; those who would love to, those who would never dream of it if they had all eternity. See how fast the two halves split and fall away when you mention you ride a motorcycle. Side one: Really? Oh, I've always wanted to ride one! Side two: Really? It's so *dangerous*."

My colleagues at work were simply in the latter camp, and I knew I needed to help them understand why the risk was worth it to me.

People who ride motorcycles, of course, are well aware of the dangers. Trust me. We all understand the risks associated with flying down the highway with little more than a helmet and some leather to protect us from a close encounter with the pavement. As we soak in the beauty of the surroundings, we're always looking out for the things that easily could take us into a slide—things you don't think about when driving on four wheels.

Pierson has a list: "wet leaves, gravel, sand, decreasing-radius turns, painted lines, tar patches liquefying in the sun, antifreeze, oil deposits at gas stations or toll booths, metal plates and manhole covers made deadly by rain, a beam falling from the back of a truck, heavy wind on a bridge. Or a greater hazard than these, which waits in primal innocence for a rear tire to send sideways in a blur: horse manure." When you're on a motorcycle, risks are around every corner.

Motorcyclists know we have to identify and manage the risks if we're going to enjoy our journey and make it success-fully, and safely, to our destination. But we embrace the risks. If we totally avoid them, we'll get much less from the experience and never reach some pretty fabulous places. This is something my team has come to understand about me over time and why I love to ride.

It's part of the thrill of why I ride. It's risky. But it's reward-ing, like becoming a parent, or being an entrepreneur, or leading a team. Yes, this is another way riding a motorcycle is very much like leadership. You can't fully enjoy the rewards if you aren't willing to take some risks.

Unfortunately, too many leaders I see are unwilling to met-aphorically jump on the bike and feel the wind in their faces, because all they see are the risks. So they don't go very far and neither do the people they lead. They end up limiting their des-tinations, and they don't experience the joy of the journey.

Others set up themselves and their organizations to take advantage of opportunities largely because they've learned how to embrace the challenging but exhilarating risks in life.

Frankly, I've come to believe one of the most dangerous risks any modern leader can take is to embrace the status quo. Leaders who aren't innovating, in fact, are risking everything. They just don't realize it. But here's the reality: We work in a constantly evolving business environment, and the competition isn't sitting still. And that competition is all around us. Indeed, the competition might not be from our industry. It might even be a start-up some teenager is launching from her parent's garage.

Consider how companies like Uber disrupted the taxi industry, or how Redbox and Netflix shook up home movie rentals. Or look at a snapshot of the camera industry. Kodak, for decades one of the world's most recognized brands, actually invented the first digital camera in 1975, but didn't market the new technology. Why? It didn't want to cannibalize its dom-inance in the film business. By the time it joined the digital revolution, it found itself chasing Sony and Canon.

Avi Dan, a contributor to *Forbes*, points out that Kodak made the classic mistake of not asking the right questions. Thus it focused on marketing and selling products rather than remembering that it was in the storytelling business not the film business.

"When Kodak decided to get in the game it was too late," Dan writes. "The company saw its market share decline, as digital imaging became dominant. . . . Kodak failed to adapt to a new marketplace and new consumer attitudes."[1]

Risk is essential for every leader in every industry. Risk takes you into the future and helps ensure your company remains relevant even while everything around you is changing. Daunting, yes. But here's the good news: taking risks is a perfect fit for anyone looking to merge destination leadership with a journey mindset. Destination leadership drives you toward risk because you know it's the only way to reach any worthy goal. A journey mindset frees you to enjoy the experience, regardless of the uncertainty. You don't have to know if everything will work. You're even OK with some failure, because you know you can learn from those experiences, and ultimately those failures lead to progress. The conflict between destination leadership and a journey mindset is actually an illusion, because merging the two is the best way to drive forward.

The thing about risk is that it often requires a counterintuitive approach, much like navigating a motorcycle. Not only do you have to "look through the turn," but you have to deftly employ something called countersteering: as you approach a turn, you briefly turn the bike in the opposite direction of the way you want to go to initiate and complement your lean.

The physics of this are complicated. They involve camber thrust, roll angle, and centripetal force. But the reality of it is simple: if you are driving down the road and push the handlebar with your right hand, the bike will lean to the right, allowing you to negotiate a right-hand turn.

Think "Steer left. Turn right." It's counterintuitive, but it's the key to riding through the turn and maneuvering a 500-pound bike to take you forward. So you have to free yourself of your fears and take the risk.

An Opportunity Mentality

Risk is risky because it takes time and money, which are always in short supply. It requires us to look outside of our industry, outside of our comfort zones, and away from the "urgent" business needs of the day. It asks us to fix what's sometimes not broken (yet) or acknowledge that our products, processes, and solutions might not be good enough for the future. It challenges us to face our fear of failure. And it's just downright uncomfortable.

All of those reasons for avoiding risks amount to one thing: an excuse for keeping the bike parked in the garage. Whenever I've given in to the temptations and excuses that squash risk, it's always held me and my company back. For example, on some occasions we've passed on making strategic hires that might have helped us start up a new service area better or faster than we could do on our own. In hindsight I could see it would have been smarter to take the risk. Only when we were willing to think and act counterintuitively—when we were willing to steer left to turn right—were we able to find new destinations and truly enjoy our journey.

A good friend of mine, Kara Trott, is the CEO of Quantum Health, a company that has become a disruptive force in the health care benefits industry largely because Kara has learned to embrace risks and innovate while others around her are content with staying parked in their garages. Some sectors of health care are highly innovative, but the benefits sector isn't one of them. In fact, Kara says it actually has a "bias against innovation." It's dominated by a few very large insurance providers who focus primarily on things like payment methodology and operational efficiencies rather than the patient's experience and journey.

"Their interest is in maintaining the status quo," Kara told me. "At their core, they're transactional machines. Operational efficiency is their model. Taking risks tends to muck up the works."

Quantum Health innovates by finding ways to relate to health care's ultimate customers: the patients and their families. But in an industry that avoids risks, this has taken patience on Kara's part and a commitment to sticking with a counterintuitive approach.

That's not easy. Kara has what I call an "opportunity mentality" that's common among leaders who embrace risks and pursue risk. You don't have to be a thrill-seeker or an adrenalin junky to take risks and innovate, but you do have to discover the freedom that comes with taking responsible chances that will allow you to grow as a leader and position you and your organization for success.

Leaders with an opportunity mentality create organizations with an opportunity mentality. When organizations operate with an opportunity mentality, they create a culture that turns risks into rewards. So let's look at some ways leaders can discover and embrace this approach.

First, Unlock Your Limits

One of the biggest reasons leaders don't take risks is that they become prisoners of their perceived limitations.

For instance, many leaders too often see innovation as something that mainly happens with technology or science. But no matter what industry or business you're in, you can try new things with products, services, proprietary processes, or methodologies. You can also change *how* you do business—finance, team structures, accessibility, and engagement styles. It's not just launching a new capability. Think about the way you serve clients or how you manage workflow or how your teams are structured; any ideas that enhance your organization's ability to cut costs, drive revenue, or grow net income are chances to innovate.

Many people are also prone to see risk as expensive—something only possible for organizations with big research and development budgets. However, when you look around the world, historically and currently, you see that necessity, curiosity, courage, and persistence are what really drive new thinking.

I was at a conference in Chicago where one of the speakers was Navi Radjou, a coauthor of *Jugaad Innovation* and *Frugal Innovation*. Those two books describe how to take smart risks and make use of available resources to drive change. Radjou says a *jugaad* is an "innovative fix or simple work-around." Innovation is not about how many resources you have, he says, but how resourceful you are with what you have. I couldn't agree more.

You also need to embrace risk as your job. It's up to you as a leader to think about the potential of your business, not just what it looks like today. When you're too busy *working in the business*, you're not *working on it*. The more you can lift your head up from your work and look over the horizon, the more astute you become at connecting the dots and finding opportunity. This is an essential skill of a leader: it's "looking through the turn" at its finest. Obviously you get better with practice.

Second, Stay Loose

Whenever you commit to taking risks, you will encounter unexpected bumps and changes in the road. When that happens during a motorcycle ride, I can't stiffen up or I'll risk losing control of my bike. The same is true as a leader. We have to expect the unexpected, be ready to go with it when it happens, stay loose, and make adjustments to keep moving forward.

When something comes along that's a threat to the business—a new competitor or a low-cost alternative—a first instinct is to wave it off, dismiss it, or stiff-arm it. However, rather than wasting time and energy defending the threat, it sometimes can be better to take a counterintuitive approach and figure out how to leverage the threat to your benefit. You might find ways to work with the competitor or develop new products or solutions that build off the low-cost alternative.

I've found the key to staying loose when navigating risks is to take the time to listen to my intuition. This isn't easy for a results-driven person like myself, because it requires slowing down and focusing on things other than the pressing issue of the day, like the changing colors of the trees on a fall ride or the fog silently floating above a river on a morning run. These moments help you clear your head and free you to see things in ways you otherwise couldn't.

Carl Honoré, the author of *In Praise of Slowness*, put it this way: "Your best ideas, those eureka moments that turn the world upside down, seldom come when you're juggling emails, rushing to meet the 5 P.M. deadline or straining to make your voice heard in a high-stress meeting. They come when you're walking the dog, soaking in the bath, or swinging in a hammock."[2]

Third, Create a Culture of Try

Trust me, your team and your clients want you to try new things. Employees are empowered by a "let's do it" mentality. Customers and clients want to know you can take them places they've never been and can't get to on their own.

Leaders need to create a "greenhouse" environment that encourages teams to try new things and see what works without fear of punishment or embarrassment if it fails. Ultimately, you want a culture that's not afraid to fail—it's afraid not to try. This is part attitude, of course, but it's also part process.

In other words, leaders first have to inspire people to try new things, encouraging them on the front end and rewarding effort regardless of the outcomes. That doesn't mean all failures are "OK," but employees should have a clear vision for what's acceptable and what's not so they aren't walking on eggshells.

One way to create a culture of try is to ask yourself and your team "how might we" questions. Each word in that phrase is important. I'm a big fan of leading through asking rather than always telling, and I particularly like this simple but powerful approach for creative problem-solving developed by Warren Berger.[3] You can open your mind to possibilities by starting the conversation in this way. The "how" part assumes there are solutions out there, and it gives creative confidence to the group—yes, we can find an answer. "Might" says we can put ideas out there that might or might not work, but either is okay when we are in brainstorming mode. Of course, the "we" is that we are going to figure it out together.

You can also put into place some simple processes that will enable and empower employees to try new ideas. The Design Council's Double Diamond[4] is a practical model used by industries and companies around the world. It involves four steps: discover, define, develop, and deliver.

In the early part of ideation, teams think broadly during the discovery phase, clarifying what the issues and opportunities are. They bring it back to a definition, identify what they're solving for, and establish a design brief. Then the process goes back outward again for development of ideas, coming back to a close at the delivery stage. The finished concept can be tested and possibly recycled around the diamond once again. It's not only a design process, but a model for improvement.

The hardest part of the Double Diamond model? Getting your team to "turn the corner": to stop brainstorming and start refining and deciding on the final product. But good leaders know how to take ideas from concept to execution, getting things across the finish line.

A culture of try, however, also needs a process that sets teams up for success and helps them mitigate failure. For instance, you can establish an in-house "labs" initiative or work closely with a local accelerator or start-up incubator to get access to entrepreneurs who are creating new things. This provides a safe, formal structure for exploring and taking risks, and it sends a message that taking risks is encouraged and rewarded.

A study in 2015 by the Altimeter Group looked at 200 large companies and found that 38 percent had set up innovation centers, mostly in Silicon Valley, with the goal of "leveraging the ecosystem of start-ups, venture capitalists, accelerators, vendors, and academic institutions that these hubs provide."[5] While most of these centers focus on technology, they also focus heavily on understanding the needs, expectations, and behaviors of customers.

This might seem like an out-of-reach idea for smaller organizations, but any group can establish a "lab," especially by partnering with others who are interested in figuring out the future together. For instance, I've been a part of a local angel investor community that listens and gives feedback to entrepreneurs who are pitching their business for funding. From that group, many more seasoned leaders have begun mentoring these new CEOs on how to grow their companies. In exchange, they give us a window into their thinking and how they envision changing their industry.

Whatever systems or processes you use, make "test and learn" a part of your culture. Experiment to see what might happen. Run parallel pilots of your most viable options. David Maister, a widely respected consultant's consultant and former professor at Harvard Business School, points out that, "Innovation wins through its portfolio of experiments, not by being super-geniuses at spotting in advance the one that is going to work. So you need to stimulate a large number of experiments."[6]

If this is all new to your culture, start with small innovation projects that have a chance to pay off early—small-scale, quick payback projects. Getting early wins will help build the confidence, change the culture, and over time, create a larger and longer-lasting impact.

Approaching risks with the right mindset is the first piece of creating an environment where innovation can flourish. It takes courage to steer left to turn right, because it feels counterintuitive. But we have to free our mind of that fear if we want to make the turn and move toward our destination.

Once we do, however, we still have to make some critical decisions like "What risks should we take?" and "How do we successfully manage them?" Although we need to be willing to take risks to innovate and grow, not all risks are created equal. When we come to the fork in the road, we need to make a wise decision about which path to take.

The Road Ahead

REVIEW

Taking risks as a leader often requires a counterintuitive approach. Just like countersteering to navigate a motorcycle, you have to steer left to turn right. Having a journey mindset as a destination leader frees you to take risks and innovate so you can stay ahead of your competition. Leading with an opportunity mentality helps you make that happen:

1. Unlock your limits.
2. Stay loose.
3. Create a culture of try.

REFLECT

- Which of Melissa Holbrook Pierson's two groups do you naturally fall into: those who do or those who don't? Why? What does this mean to your future as a leader?
- How would adopting more of a journey mindset free you to take more risk?
- What is the potential for your job, team, or business 10 years from now?

CHAPTER 8

The Fork in the Road

Several popular YouTube videos show a motorcyclist speeding down a narrow path of a mountain, a path so narrow, in fact, that in some places it's not much wider than his tires. As you watch the view from the biker's helmet-mounted GoPro camera, you can't help noticing that the slightest error on the rider's part will send him and the bike crashing down the steep cliff. Of course, he makes it safely down the mountain, sometimes throwing in a backflip off a ramp along the way.[1]

While I would love the thrill of doing this trick myself, I'm smart enough to know I'd never be able to pull that off and stay in one piece. I keep to the highway, which actually provides plenty of its own thrills. But as I pointed out in the previous chapter, no matter what your risk threshold, whether on a bike or as a leader of your business, you have to go outside your comfort zone if you want to go to interesting places and accomplish extraordinary things. The reality is, most risks don't require the death-defying acts we see in extreme sports. They require courage to go somewhere new, but the wisdom to go there in the right way. When courage and wisdom align, we give ourselves a chance to innovate and make the risks we take pay off for us and our teams.

Innovation can seem daunting and complex, but at its core, it's simply about turning ideas into money. The trick is to find the right opportunities that fit you and your business. In other words, it's about evaluating and managing risks.

At Mitchell Communications, we've been early-to-market with a number of new offerings, for example creative services, because we believed the risk made sense for us and we had a strong right to win. At other times, we've stepped back to watch something develop before deciding whether to jump in. And at times we've passed on a risk altogether.

Most leaders have no shortage of grand ideas, and you may find yourself surrounded by idea people. That's great. But as leaders, we have to learn to say "yes" only to the best. Believe me, I can think of a hundred things I'd like to try, but most of them should never see the light of day. I've learned the value of censoring my constant flow of ideas and focusing on the areas where I have the greatest opportunity to succeed.

That's easier said than done, you might say. Maybe. But it doesn't have to be as difficult as we often make it. I use some pretty simple criteria, first linked together by IDEO[2] to help define the sweet spot for innovation, that I think works across all industries. I try to adopt the opportunity mentality we talked about in the previous chapter and look for opportunities within the intersection of the following:

- Desirability—is it wanted or needed?
- Feasibility—can we do it?
- Viability—can we make money?

These three criteria, allow you to think through things like the cost, the potential for increased revenues, profitability, how an idea might work in the marketplace, how it fits with your current and future strategies, and how you will measure success. Then when you arrive at the fork in the road, you can make a wise decision about which way to go.

Desirability: Reading the Signs

When I am riding down the road on a motorcycle, I am constantly looking and listening to what is happening around me. That includes the highway signs, of course, but some of the most important signs aren't posted by the highway department. They are in the sights. They're in the smells. They're in the sounds. They're often mystical and sometimes cryptic.

The same is true when we're evaluating risks as a business leader. To know if a risk is worth taking, we have to know if our idea is wanted or needed. We seldom see a sign on the Interstate saying, "Go this way!" So to figure out if the idea is desirable, we have to understand our changing world. When we watch and listen to the world around us, we can spot trends, understand them better, and anticipate changes that are coming our way—all keys to managing risk and driving innovation. This is how we prepare to answer the always important question: Is there a market for my great idea? It's how we identify the right ideas to fit the market.

Where should you look for ideas and trends? Everywhere. Listen to your children. Hire a teenager to spend an hour or two each month teaching you something he or she knows how to do.

Glean insights from your hobbies, from family members, from friends. Read magazines and blogs across a broad spectrum of industries. Invite diverse thinking into your conversations, and look at things from a broad point of view. Fill your talent pool with people from different backgrounds and experiences.

Kara Trott, the CEO from Quantum Health whom I referenced in the previous chapter, is a rare bird in her industry because she hasn't spent her entire career in health care or insurance benefits. She started in retail and is a lawyer by trade. Her "outsider" perspective is a competitive advantage. So she cultivates it by proactively looking in unlikely and unusual places in search of new ideas that are worth trying.

"A lot of innovation isn't radically new thinking," Kara told me. "It's taking things that worked in other areas and figuring out a different application from that. Or it's organic. Maybe you can't develop something in your industry until you see something that was developed in another industry. It's like the space program. So much technology came out of the space program that wasn't applicable there but was applicable to packaging, food growth and preservation, and other industries. Some people think you have to invent something that doesn't exist, and that's not true."

You likely will miss the most important signs along the road if you conform to "confirmation bias" where you read or listen only to sources that support your existing views. As F. Scott Fitzgerald said, "The test of a first-rate intelligence is the ability to hold two opposed ideas in the mind at the same time, and still retain the ability to function."[3]

When you open your mind and look around, you can spot the trends that will inform the risks you take and the innovations you pursue. You'll know what employees, customers, clients, vendors, and shareholders really want and need, then you can pursue it.

As children we all learned to play a simple game that created something from nothing; we started with an unrecognizable collection of dots, but when we drew lines between them, an image or pattern emerged. Connect-the-dots is a simple concept for child's play, but do not be fooled by its simplicity. The same holds true in innovation. When we are faced with things that are unfamiliar, disorganized, even chaotic, we can make sense of them by drawing lines in just the right places and discovering new ideas as a result. Sometimes we even have to be willing to let go of the picture we thought would emerge or that we wanted to draw, and go with something totally different.

Consider how your world might look differently if you had spotted some trends sooner. For instance, one of the biggest trends today involves the emergence of the "sharing economy." This is the Internet-driven phenomenon that allows people to rent rooms from each other or share a ride or borrow power tools, and it's become big business for companies like Airbnb and Uber.

Airbnb, for instance, had a market valuation of $20 billion in late 2015, but it was founded in 2008 by a couple of people in California who decided to rent a spare room to strangers as a creative way to pay their rent. It took a few years, but Airbnb took off because of smart decisions that took advantage of marketplace trends like the growth of social media and people's desire to buy locally and direct.

What could you or I have done differently in 2008 when we had seen this trend emerging? We could have talked to consumers who were using it, asked them why and what they liked about it. Listening to outliers helps us gain a different perspective from the accepted wisdom of the day. Seeing the trend early would have positioned us to innovate in our own world, because it would have helped us understand where the world was heading and therefore what was wanted or needed. Then we could more accurately evaluate the risks of doing something, or nothing, in response to those changes.

When I'm reading the signs to determine desirability, I try to do it in light of my needs, my organization's needs, and our clients' needs. An innovation expert once told me, "Obnoxious clients give you the future." We don't have obnoxious clients, of course, but I know what he meant. Clients who challenge you with their problems and don't let you rest on your laurels are helping you understand where you need to grow as a company. Once you learn their pain points, you can identify a solution and determine if this is a one-off or if other clients have the same pain point. Your solution to their need just might become a service you can scale.

Feasibility: Knowing Thyself

Just because there's a market for an idea doesn't mean we should pursue it immediately or at all. Some risks aren't worth taking, simply because the idea isn't feasible. Some risks require front-end investments to make success feasible.

When I spoke with Kara about how they innovate at Quantum Health, she pointed out that most people think the idea is the innovation when really the innovation is in the execution.

"Ideas without execution are worthless," she said. "A C-idea executed at an A-level is better than an A-idea executed at a C-level."

When I think about barriers to execution, I often start with a seemingly unrelated question: "Will someone buy this from us?" I'm not asking if someone wants or needs what I'm offering. We've already addressed that. Now I'm asking if they will actually pull the trigger and "buy" it. If not, why not? What's the barrier to execution? What's the barrier to feasibility?

The question holds true regardless of whether the customer is internal or external. If we can't deliver—or even if the customer believes we can't deliver—when and where it's needed, at the right price, and at the appropriate level of quality, then they won't buy what we're offering. If they won't buy it, then the risk doesn't pass the feasibility test. This helps unlock all sorts of reasons why something isn't feasible: we don't have the right people or enough people, we don't have the necessary equipment, we don't have the infrastructure, we don't have access to the right vendors, or, and this is one leaders often miss, we don't have the credibility.

I might have a great service idea, for instance, but the world might not see me as a credible provider of that particular service. The world might question my credentials or my experience or my expertise—and the world might be right. If our public relations agency suddenly announced we were going to sell a new line of innovative auto parts, no one would take us seriously. In an extreme example like that, I'd definitely drop the idea. But if the idea is good enough—like offering training services to our clients—I might invest in building credibility so we're not seen as a pretender. Or if we're already better positioned than others because of our unique expertise and track record, I might invest in telling our story so people realize we have the chops to deliver what they want or need.

The feasibility test often comes down to whether the risk is a natural extension of our core business. Lego is a great example of this. The famed toy block maker nearly went under in 2003, mainly because it veered so far from its core business. In an effort to compete with video games and other tech-driven toys, Lego was creating cartoons, manufacturing larger (non-Lego-like) blocks, marketing customized kits of Legos, and opening theme parks.

The company returned to sound footing by refocusing on its basic blocks, but that doesn't mean it's not trying new things. In fact, Lego's "Future Lab" intentionally focuses on understanding what children want and how to deliver it in cool, fun new ways that fit within Lego's core businesses.

Viability: Determining Your ROI

Remember, innovation is about turning ideas into money. The discussion about risk always circles back to finances, so you have to determine your return on investment (ROI).

The age-old business axiom "follow the money" rings true here. Before you introduce an idea into the marketplace, you need to examine who is willing to pay to bring the idea to life. You don't want to be an idea in search of a market.

You might find a huge group that loves your idea but doesn't have the money. Or maybe they have the money but they can't get to it quickly because their organization is a bureaucratic mess. Or maybe they love your idea but think it would disrupt their status quo and they fear change. Ultimately, you have to find funding (customers, investors, etc.) whose interests align with what you can offer and who can provide the funding you need. That, by the way, might be the funding you need to get started, not to build your dream version. There are times when you have to innovate in stages, as each risk yields a reward.

Ultimately, every risk needs to deliver a return. You might even decide that you're okay with a financial loss because the return provides something greater. For instance, we made a conscious decision as we began rapidly growing to invest heavily in our people. I firmly believe things like 100 percent employer-paid health care, in-house trainings, and other benefits I mentioned in Chapter 6 helped us recruit and retain our talent. But to fund these initiatives, we needed the rest of our business to be highly profitable. And I needed to feel strongly about the ROI.

ROI is critical no matter what type of risk you're taking. I have often asked myself: if we invest this much money in getting something started, how long before we make our money back and make a profit? It's the starting point for figuring out the best use of our money: where to invest, for how long, and for what return.

I wasn't a financial expert when I started my firm, but I knew how important it was to run a fiscally sound business and I figured it out along the way. Today, I understand the finer points of GAAP (generally accepted accounting principles), which doesn't make me a very interesting dinner date, but it has helped me do a better job of running a profitable enterprise.

As a leader, you need to be grounded in the fundamentals of finance. You've got to understand and appreciate practical principles like interpreting financial statements and leveraging key drivers in the business. If you're looking for ways to enhance your financial savvy, I recommend *Finance for Executives: Managing for Value Creation* by Gabriel Hawawini and Claude Viallet, attending a class on finance, or if nothing else, asking a CPA to spend a half-day giving you a crash course on the basics. A good grasp of finance will empower you to make smarter business decisions and to have a better feel for how to place your bets for your particular situation.

Willing to Fail

When I speak on innovation, I often ask the audience members this question: What if I were one of the investors on the TV show *Shark Tank*, and I gave you $100,000 to drive growth in your business? How would you invest it? At Mitchell, we've always prioritized investing in both talent and technology. As a professional services business, we believe the magic comes from the intersection of the two.

Our foray into video provides a nice example. In 2009, we mainly outsourced whatever we did with video. It wasn't a core strength for us or for agencies like ours. We faced a fork in the road. Should we continue to outsource or innovate by making video a core strength? There were risks involved, but ultimately we decided to launch a video team, and here's why:

- We read the signs and saw that it was something our clients wanted and needed, and they were willing to spend money on it.

- The rise of social media opened new options for where we could use videos—on new platforms such as Facebook and in more interactive websites that companies were moving toward to enhance their online presence.
- The response to our early work in video had been positive; clients liked our work.
- We looked at the market and found capable and available local talent.
- The price for high-definition equipment was dropping, making that part of the investment significantly more affordable.

All of that led us to believe the idea was desirable, feasible, and viable.

We invested about $100,000 and made that back in the very first year. Today we're producing more than 300 different video projects annually with five full-time and part-time employees who work with all of the bells and whistles of a first-class video studio.

Was it a risk? Sure. There are no guarantees in life. But we were aware of the emerging opportunities, determined it made sense, and had the courage to pull the trigger.

Public relations is our core business, but today we are an integrated communications firm. We started our creative department in 2009 and moved quickly into video. We also have significant offerings around digital and social media, influencer marketing, Web technology, consumer insights, and training and development. This is where our industry is headed, and I'm glad we took some risk to establish these services along the way.

We've always been willing to take some calculated risks to establish new services that were quite different from other agencies. Sometimes it worked, sometimes it didn't. For example, we tried to launch a research department several years ago that never took off for a variety of reasons, and critically the budgets we had secured for that team were shifting to other more pressing needs. So as painful as it was, we closed down that group, went back to the drawing board, and listened more.

What did clients want and need? As it turns out, it was insights rather than research. They wanted data-driven answers to the questions "So what?" and "Now what?" So we created a consumer insights team that actually drives our entire strategy and creative process. They have helped position us as strategic communications counselors, not just creative thinkers or excellent executors.

We wanted to be seen as trusted advisors playing at a high level with our clients. We did that by bringing insight and understanding, as well as all the new communications services they wanted and needed. But we only got there by freeing ourselves up to try different ideas.

Our approach to innovation then and now requires a dual mindset where we are equally skilled at inspiring people and encouraging big-picture thinking while also demonstrating the financial acumen needed to drive revenue and grow profits. The right mix allows us to enjoy the ride and reach the places we want to go.

The Road Ahead

REVIEW

Every idea we come up with isn't worth pursuing. In fact, some really good ideas aren't worth pursuing. To innovate successfully, the trick is to learn to evaluate the risks and take the right ones at the right time. Innovation happens when you look for opportunities within the intersection of the following:

- Desirability—is it wanted or needed?
- Feasibility—can we do it?
- Viability—can we make money?

REFLECT

- Think of a time you tried something and it didn't work. What did you learn?
- How well do you execute? Is there a C-level idea you could execute at an A-level right now that would help move your business forward?
- How are you currently evaluating risks that might make your company more innovative?

CHAPTER 9

Moving Full Speed

"And the winner is . . . Mitchell Communications Group!"

I was never more stunned to hear those words than on the night of March 10, 2011. Our entire leadership team was sitting in a ballroom in midtown Manhattan with a thousand other leaders at the annual *PR Week* Awards banquet. This is like the Oscars in our industry. Winning hardware on this night puts you on a very short list of top agencies and corporations in the competitive world of communications. Being named as an Agency of the Year is like winning Best Picture—many want it, few ever get it.

There we were, a group of hardworking public relations (PR) pros who hadn't slept much in the past few years. We had been building Mitchell and trying to keep our arms around the burgeoning agency. Despite our rapid growth—more than 400 percent in four years, at this point—I had been hesitant to throw our hat in the ring for these sorts of things. But a nearly three-hour breakfast conversation with a key industry leader a year or so earlier changed all that.

I met Julia Hood in late 2009 when she was the publishing director of *PRWeek* magazine. She's now an executive vice president and chief content officer for Haymarket Media, *PRWeek*'s parent company, and in 2015 she added global brand director to her title. Over the years, she has proven herself as an exceptional writer, someone who is straightforward in her analysis of things, and a respected advocate who is always driving the industry forward. In short, there are many reasons why I would want to know her, but in 2009, I wasn't sure why she would want to meet me.

Michael Lasky, my lawyer since the early 2000s, introduced us. Michael is also a force in the industry. He is cochair of the litigation practice group of Davis & Gilbert law firm in New York, but he is known in PR circles for his deep expertise and specialization in counseling owners of PR, advertising, and other professional service firms.

Michael had been urging me for a few years to become more active in the industry on a national level, but I didn't think I had the time or, frankly, a big enough firm or good enough story to earn that right. When I finally agreed for Michael to introduce me to Julia, I had no idea how that meeting would change our approach to thought leadership and reshape my personal leadership journey.

Julia and I sat at a small table in Pershing Square, a restaurant on 42nd Street directly across the street from Grand Central Station. After we ordered coffee and introduced ourselves, she asked me to tell her about my agency. I went back to the beginning, telling her how Raye and I had moved to Northwest Arkansas in 1995 and how I had started the agency basically at my kitchen table. I told her about building the virtual network of talent, and how we had acquired Walmart, Tyson, J.B. Hunt, Sam's Club, and Southwestern Energy as major national clients. I told her about moving into two different offices to accommodate our growing full-time staff, which was then up to about 17 people, and how we had bought a training and facilitation business the year prior. I also told her we were hoping to top $3 million in revenue by the end of that year.

My story went long and included far more details than anyone besides me would really want to know. But Julia's response was simply this: "How come I've never met you before?" She was absolutely surprised to hear our story and pleased to discover an agency that didn't fit the traditional mold.

Julia told me the industry needed fresh voices and the size of the firm didn't define its value. She urged me to raise my hand to be a guest speaker and writer when the magazine had opportunities and to enter our work in the *PRWeek* Awards.

That second suggestion caught my attention, because it was something we could do right away. But to do it, we would literally have to do it *right away*. When I got back to the firm the following Monday, I told our leadership team I wanted to enter. They were excited . . . until they learned we had only until Friday to get it done! But we all agreed that with the growth and momentum the agency was experiencing, now was the time to try and we would do whatever it took to get the entry finished and shipped to New York before the deadline.

We were eligible for the Boutique Agency category, which was anything less than $5 million in gross revenue. The judges included notable industry leaders, and I knew we'd be up against stiff competition. We would have to tell a compelling story and produce an outstanding entry, and our team did an amazing job.

We found out we were a finalist for Agency of the Year a few months later. Michael Clark and I decided to fly our small leadership team to New York for the event. We didn't win, but being in the ballroom that night and seeing close-up the quality of work and the level of excellence that other agencies and corporations were achieving only made me want it more. We were thrilled to be there, but I wasn't satisfied. I set my sights on winning the next time.

Fast-forward one year later to March 10, 2011, and there we sat, surprised and delighted—and winners of the award for Small Agency of the Year. (We had grown and moved into the category for agencies between $5 million and $10 million.) A few minutes later, Mitchell won a second award: honorable mention for the overall Agency of the Year as one of the best agencies regardless of size.

Taking home two prestigious awards that night was a special moment for our team, which had worked so hard for so many years to build a truly exceptional firm in the most unlikely of places. Unbeknownst to us, it was just the beginning of a string of honors the agency would earn over the next few years as we increased our efforts around thought leadership.

Worth It? Or Not?

When you begin to soar as a leader, you often are asked to share your knowledge and expertise. This can be a gratifying part of a leader's journey, and it's how you become what is commonly referred to as a thought leader. Thought leaders are recognized for their competence, their passion for what they do, and their compelling point of view. They share their ideas freely and are respected for their contributions to their industry and to the broader business community.

It sounds great, but wading into these waters can be a little scary. When the requests escalate to include speaking, writing, and other more visible engagements, perhaps even on a national stage, deciding what to pursue can become challenging and confusing. This is especially true for those who are unsure about how and why to become more visible in the first place.

Is it worth the effort and the cost (in time and money) to become a thought leader? Or is it just a distraction—something that takes energy away from the "real" work of running a business?

I believe it is worth it, if it's done the right way. A thought leadership platform works best when it's carefully planned and implemented. Like anything else, a solid strategy for focusing your resources increases your chances of getting solid ROI. But thought leadership looks different, depending upon several factors, including your personality as a leader, your industry, and the stage of your journey (as a leader and as an organization).

Like the agency itself, our approach to thought leadership at Mitchell developed over time until we intentionally ramped up our efforts following my meeting with Julia in 2009. So wherever you are in your leadership or organizational journey, there are always things you can do to develop your potential as a thought leader.

As a young professional, for instance, I was very active as a volunteer in the PR industry and in my local community. My primary professional efforts were with the Public Relations

Society of America (PRSA) and the International Association of Business Communicators. I served as a leader in each organization: in the local chapters, on regional district boards, and on national committees. I also served on several local nonprofit and civic boards, usually as the communications or special events chair.

I loved meeting other leaders and learning new skills such as large-scale project management, leading other leaders, and setting and achieving stretch goals. I also had a few unsolicited job offers, which underscored the value of networking and demonstrating your expertise to a broader audience.

When we moved to Northwest Arkansas, I stayed involved with PRSA, spearheading the effort to establish a chapter in the region. I also expanded my involvement to include local, regional, and statewide business organizations, as well as several well-regarded nonprofit and civic groups. I served on boards and expanded my personal and professional networks significantly, earning dear friends and many clients along the way. I also began writing guest columns for the local business journal and speaking at business events.

Expanding Our Efforts

As the agency grew, other leaders on the team started speaking and writing, as well. It wasn't uncommon for people to call our office looking for any of the talented Mitchell team to participate in a business or civic activity. In 2009 when we put a more intentional and focused strategy behind our thought leadership, things really took off.

Several people on our leadership team drove agency involvement in prominent business and civic organizations by serving on boards or in other key leadership roles. We also joined several national women's associations in the retail and consumer packaged goods (CPG) industries. And I continued to drive our industry involvement nationally.

In the fall of 2011, I met Paul Holmes, the founder of *The Holmes Report* and more than a dozen media outlets, events, awards, and recognition programs. Paul is another major force in our industry, and I was delighted to share the Mitchell story with him, but also nervous as all get-out. As it turned out, there was no reason to be. Paul loves a great entrepreneurial story, and he had the same reaction Julia did, wondering why we had never met before.

Over the next two years, *The Holmes Report* named us Small Agency of the Year and ranked us as one of the ten fastest growing agencies globally (at this point we had grown more than 500 percent in five years). We saw firsthand the powerful reach *The Holmes Report* had with corporate clients in the industry, as these recognitions were noted by many clients and prospects who talked with us afterward.

Our partnership with *PRWeek* also continued, and I increased my involvement with industry groups like the PR Council and PRSA Counselors Academy. One of the reasons I loved my leadership experiences with industry organizations was because I learned so much from other agency leaders about the challenges and opportunities they faced. Working with them on solutions not only helped them, but also helped me stay on top of how the industry was changing and led me to think about ways we could continue to evolve Mitchell.

In short, our agency has been able to have a big voice in an industry that had in many ways grown deaf to small and mid-size agencies.

"You changed that perspective in our industry," Julia told me. "So the lesson for other leaders is this: find people in your industry who will listen to you. Seek them out, because they won't necessarily find you. People have their circles, and they can become echo chambers. Change the conversation by being part of it."

Creating a Platform

We created a thought leadership platform partly in response to the demand that resulted from our growth and partly as a strategy for continuing our growth. But creating that platform wasn't easy. It was great that we were growing and that people wanted to know more about our story, but how should we go about it? How could we manage it all and keep the business running?

Not every opportunity to speak, write, or participate was the best use of our time. Plus we were all working nonstop to take care of our clients, which was always our first priority. How should we make choices about what invitations to accept and which ones to say no to? How should we decide if and when to get involved on a national level? And what practical steps did we need to make to ensure we got a return on our investments of time, energy, and, of course, money?

As we began to craft a strategy, we kept in mind some fundamentals that any leader can apply when thinking through a program. Here are some of the valuable lessons we learned as we created and implemented the strategy.

Study What's Out There

One of the first things you can do is figure out what other organizations are doing in your industry and in your community and how well they're doing it. In other words, do some homework. Look at the issues in the marketplace and what's on the minds of your clients. Study other successful thought leadership programs and identify what is working.

At Mitchell, we determined what types of influencers we wanted to reach and we put a master list together. It included not only clients, but also prospects, elected officials, leaders of business and industry associations, key reporters and contacts in the media, members of many important nonprofit boards, and other select agency friends.

Your research will help you set specific goals for a thought leadership plan. Ours included goals around greater visibility for the agency, a desirable positioning in our areas of expertise, a stronger ability to attract top talent to work for us, new clients and a more diversified revenue stream, and increased morale among the entire team.

Identify Your Spokespersons

Who on your team has a passion and a point of view worth sharing, as well as the credibility to back it up? Often, of course, this is the founder or CEO, but you can have spokespersons at all levels. Look across your leadership ranks to find those who can authentically and boldly share new ideas and can engage stakeholders in meaningful discussion about business-impacting issues.

Refine Your Message

Armed with a clear idea of what you want to accomplish, you need to develop the core messages you want to consistently communicate. For Mitchell, this included our expertise in PR, the story of our company's growth, and our commitment to advance our industry and our community through giving back.

We also developed a specific messaging strategy for me. I worked closely with two of our senior leaders at the agency, Sarah Clark and Michelle Nelson who both had great experience in developing thought leadership platforms for executives. They were the driving force behind our overall strategy, but they also strongly encouraged me to tell my leadership story. I was a little unsure how that could help the agency, but they knew an authentic and accessible leader who is willing to share her story and the lessons learned along the way would help draw additional positive attention to the company.

We developed key messages that focused on things I was most passionate about and could speak to with credibility: entrepreneurship, leadership, and building a compelling culture. This is when I first began developing the concept of the journey and the destination to describe all that had happened in my life personally and professionally.

Inspired by my newfound love of motorcycling, my inaugural talk on a national stage was in June 2011 in another midtown Manhattan ballroom to several hundred industry leaders from across the country. It was titled "Looking Through the Turn: On the Journey of Life and Leadership" and told the story of the agency I loved and what I was learning as a leader who was lucky to be on the ride of her life.

Tune Into Your Channels

Each organization is different, but nearly everyone has access to multiple channels for sharing their story. You have your website, of course, but there are tons of other earned and owned media opportunities. You just have to identify them (that's the research) and use them to connect with your key audiences.

We started by carefully selecting several national business and industry organizations we wanted to get involved with, including a few women's business groups. Sarah and Michelle developed this list, and their thinking was very valuable, particularly on the latter point. It would further refine our focus on women's entrepreneurship, a space we were obviously well suited for and had already earned some credibility. In 2007, we had become a certified women-owned business through the Women's Business Enterprise National Council (WBENC). That same year, we hosted a luncheon for about 70 women business owners to raise awareness for certification with WBENC and the regional organization, the Women's Business Council of the Southwest (WBCS). We won three different awards from WBENC and WBCS between 2008 and 2011 for our work to encourage women's entrepreneurship in the region and also for our own company's growth.

We broadened our focus to include five highly respected national organizations: Women Impacting Public Policy, the Women Presidents Organization, Enterprising Women, the National Association for Female Executives, and Working Mother Media. Michelle and I met with each organization. Our hosts were warm and welcoming, curious to hear our story, and just as encouraging as Julia and Michael had been about seeing us get involved. As we did that, we reaped the benefits.

We expanded our national network of corporate leaders and entrepreneurs, gained greater visibility by speaking at various conferences and leadership events, wrote articles and blog posts for these organizations, and received several awards.[1]

In addition to our positioning and engagement plan, we put together an editorial calendar that set topics and timelines for content creation throughout the year. For example, we prepared case studies on our best work (being careful to observe client confidentiality restrictions) and launched a digital portfolio for clients and prospects to take a virtual tour of our work. Blake Woolsey and her team at our training center created monthly webinars that were offered for free to give prospects a taste of our training capabilities. Our creative group shot a series of videos featuring our agency leaders offering insights on their areas of expertise, and we posted these on our website and the agency's YouTube channel. We drafted numerous social media posts and blog posts for our website, as well as the websites of organizations that we were members of. One year we brought in a speaker for a client summit on social media. We also drafted and distributed a few select email announcements to agency clients and friends when we had news to share or a special resource to offer.

Let me pause for a moment and address something you might be wondering: How did we find the time to get all of this done? As I mentioned in previous chapters, we had always been stretched pretty thin and had to be wise about the time and effort we were putting toward anything new. Whatever we decided to take on had to be worked in to our schedules after clients' needs had been met first.

Here are a few things that helped us pull it all off.

- Having a focus was critical so we didn't get pulled in too many directions.
- Setting some allocations for the amount of time helped prevent scope creep.
- Our staff and capacity had grown as an agency, too, so we were able to divide the workload among several of us.
- I looked for windows of my own time I could redirect toward this effort, too—for example, late in the evening after the family was settled in, getting up an hour or two early a few mornings a week, or while I was sitting on an airplane. While this might not be something you are willing to do for the long haul, taking a quick inventory of your schedule will likely reveal some "found time" you can repurpose to get an initiative like this off the ground.

Take a Stand

Look for the areas where your organization has deep expertise and differentiating capabilities, especially around issues that are important to your stakeholders. The goal is to stake out a space where you can establish a clear platform that isn't already effectively claimed by others.

If you want to stand out in all the noise that's clanging throughout the world these days, you can't waste the spotlight on the predictable. You need to find ways to challenge conventional thinking, push new ideas, and position your organization as pioneering. You can't force the issue, of course. People can easily spot a phony. But when you identify your passion points, and those shared by others in your organization, you'll find causes to adopt and champion.

For instance, as a female entrepreneur, I've always looked for ways to encourage and support other women who own their own businesses. So one of the biggest wins for our thought leadership strategy came when I testified before Congress in the summer of 2012, thanks to my work with Women Impacting Public Policy (WIPP).

The U.S. House Committee on Small Business was holding a full congressional hearing titled, "Tales of Resilience: Small Business Survival in the Recession." The committee asked WIPP to suggest a company that had succeeded despite the challenging economy of the past few years. I was on WIPP's national board at the time, and Barbara Kasoff, WIPP's founder, and Ann Sullivan, the lead lobbyist, recommended that I share the Mitchell story on this national stage.

I was deeply honored when the committee formally invited me. I used the theme "looking through the turn" and focused on the key messages we had developed in our new thought leadership strategy. My testimony[2] included an overview of our firm, clients, and the region we call home; how we have achieved growth; ways other companies can grow in spite of a still uncertain economy; and what Washington can do to help small businesses succeed.

Before and after the hearing, I met with various congressional representatives and shared highlights of my testimony. Without exception, I received tremendous support for our firm, for our industry, and for the important role the private sector plays in driving our economy.

I was the only woman testifying at the hearing and proud to represent other women entrepreneurs who are working hard to build their businesses. Women are the fastest-growing group of entrepreneurs in the United States. A report commissioned by American Express OPEN estimates there are 11.3 million women-owned firms, or 38 percent of all independent businesses in the country.[3] It was also an honor to bring positive recognition to the PR industry, and I was asked to write a blog post[4] on my experiences for the PR Council and an article for *PRWeek*.[5]

But the greatest benefit of testifying was the pride our firm's employees and clients felt by having their story told. The hearing was televised live and we had TVs on in the office so employees could watch. Many clients told us how proud they were that their agency was receiving such positive attention nationally, reinforcing their decision to place their trust in us.

This specific opportunity underscored the value of increased visibility to the firm, particularly when you can focus the messaging on those who helped you achieve success—namely your employees, your clients, your community, and your industry.

Monitor and Measure

Establishing meaningful metrics can demonstrate how thought leadership helps build your business. You can monitor indicators such as greater engagement from stakeholders, higher quality new business inquiries, requests for thought leaders to speak at preferred venues, heightened awareness of key messages and understanding of your platform issues, and ultimately, of course, a desired behavior change motivated by a call-to-action.

Our plan included measurable objectives such as the number of speaking engagements we wanted to do, the size and types of audiences we wanted to reach, specific publications we wanted to be featured in, how frequently our core messaging was included in their coverage, targeted client prospects we wanted to meet, important business and industry influencers we wanted to build relationships with, and new organizations we wanted to work with that would enable us to meet and connect with their communities.

Be patient, of course, when it comes to the results. It takes time to create and refine a compelling message and build the relationships with the right people who want and need to hear it. Building a thought leadership platform is a marathon, not a sprint. But the time and effort you invest will produce results for you and your organization over the long run.

Reaping the Rewards

So let's go back to that question I threw out earlier: Is all of this worth it? Well, we at Mitchell invested wisely in a more strategic approach to thought leadership, and I'm confident it paid off in significant benefits to the agency and to me personally. Here are few:

- **Revenue growth:** Our growth continued at a strong pace. In 2011 our revenue was $11.5 million, and by 2014 we had grown to nearly $16 million.
- **Talent:** We successfully attracted significant new talent to join the agency, including several senior-level professionals who helped us launch new practice areas. Many of these employees said the same thing in their interview: they had been watching Mitchell Communications and wanted to be part of a highly regarded and fast-growing company. The

"careers" page on our website gets more visits than any other page, and when it launched in 2012 our applications went from a couple of hundred to more than a thousand in less than a year.

- **Clients:** Our client roster continued to expand with major national accounts such as Hilton Hotels & Resorts and Procter & Gamble. These would have been much harder to land without a reputation as a nationally respected agency.

- **Trends:** Networking with colleagues and talking with industry leaders and observers gave us a more detailed view of how the PR industry was changing. We heard what others were experiencing in terms of changing client needs, where budgets were shifting, and how new influences such as procurement were impacting the agency-client relationship. These insights confirmed some of our thinking about how we wanted to grow Mitchell and stay ahead of the many changes that were coming at us.

- **Recognition:** We've won more than 40 national, statewide, or regional industry and business awards,[6] not including many other honors for our work. We've been selective about the things we wanted to win. While we haven't won everything we've tried for, we have benefited from the awards that have come our way. The media coverage and credibility enhanced the agency's reputation and brought valuable awareness to our team.

- **Greater visibility:** During the time frame when we ramped up our approach to thought leadership, articles on the agency appeared both online and in print for *PRWeek*, *The Holmes Report*, *Arkansas Business*, and the Tuck School of Business at Dartmouth and many other outlets. The exposure from articles, speeches by members of our team, and awards we won all contributed to greater visibility. For instance, visits to our website more than doubled: from 22,364 visits in 2011 to 46,497 in 2014. And engagement on our agency Facebook page nearly tripled.

- **Desirable positioning:** By listening to clients and our up-close observations of changes in the industry, we evolved our expertise in key areas such as digital and social media, Web technology, consumer insights, and content marketing. Importantly, we positioned the agency through a brand refresh in 2015 with unique expertise in three core areas: consumer marketing, hyperlocal activation, and brand reputation. This positioning led to a strong uptick in prospect inquiries and conversations with existing clients about new ways we can expand our work with them.

- **Employee morale:** While recognizing individuals for their work is important, so is making everyone feel they're a part of something bigger than themselves. When we survey our team, they overwhelmingly agree that Mitchell has a good reputation regionally and industrywide. In 2012, 93 percent of them agreed or strongly agreed with that idea, and it was up to 96 percent in 2013. And 96 percent of our team agrees or strongly agrees that they are proud to work at Mitchell. We've always had good morale at Mitchell, but I believe our thought-leadership efforts have drawn us closer as a team and allowed us to connect as we accomplished things together.

Personally, I have benefited far more than I could have imagined from our enhanced approach to thought leadership.

I met other entrepreneurs who had been hard at it like I had been for years. These leaders became some of my best friends in the business—and in life, really. And their experiences benefited us greatly. I was able to gain valuable insights and share those with our leadership team. Together we could identify ways we might apply those learnings to our situation.

While it enhanced my personal brand and profile as a leader, that really was just a side benefit. More important, I found pure joy in sharing the story of our company, my leadership journey, and the countless lessons we have learned that have made us wiser, stronger, and better. Thought leadership helped me find my voice and bring some sense to all that had happened to me. In doing so, I developed more of a journey mindset, which I desperately needed to find during the craziness of these hypergrowth years. This book has also been a part of that process. Throughout the writing of it over the past year, I have rediscovered many events that have brought back memories I will always treasure, and I am hopeful my experiences will help others.

Finally, our thought leadership led us to realize one of the most valuable opportunities an entrepreneur can have: the opportunity to consider selling your company, an experience that would put me squarely in the friction zone.

The Road Ahead

REVIEW

A strategic approach to thought leadership can give you and your organization a voice in your community and in your industry, helping you reach your destination with the satisfaction of knowing you helped others along the way. Here are some things to keep in mind when creating a strategy:

- Study what's out there.
- Identify your spokespersons.
- Refine your message.
- Tune into your channels.
- Take a stand.
- Monitor and measure.

REFLECT

- How are you viewed as a leader (a) within your organization, (b) within your community, and (c) throughout your industry? How is your organization viewed by those three groups?
- How might increasing your visibility as a thought leader help you reach your goals (personal and organizational)?

CHAPTER 10

In the Friction Zone

L earning to ride a motorcycle is a lot like learning to ride a bicycle. With both, you need a sense of balance and enough speed to stay upright as you travel down the road. But on a motorcycle, you must also learn to control the speed and power of a magnificent machine, something that happens largely in a place called the friction zone.

Susan Rzepka Orion, a writer and certified motorcycling instructor, points out that before you can make a motorcycle move smoothly, you have to "practice the fine art of clutch control" that happens in the friction zone: "the small wonder in the big world of motorcycling . . . where the clutch slips and the transmission grips, and partial power is transmitted to the rear wheel."[1] You find the friction zone on a motorcycle by using the clutch on the left-hand grip. But as Orion points out, "No one can show you its exact location. The friction zone is something you can't see. You have to feel it."[2] The journey of leadership is often like this, especially when it comes to making big decisions.

I've found we're in the heart of the friction zone when we're compelled to make life-changing decisions that impact our destination and the quality of our journey. We have momentum and balance, but we see things changing around us and we don't know whether to accelerate and go full throttle or to pull back and wait for things to engage and develop.

Decisions in the friction zone take different forms for different leaders. *Is it time for a career change? Should I start a new company? Should I buy out a competitor? Should I sell the company I founded and nurtured to maturity? Should I retire? If so, what's next?*

I've faced all of those questions, but by far the biggest decision for me was whether to sell Mitchell Communications Group. The crucial time before, during, and immediately after the sale of my company taught me several key lessons about leading an organization, which I believe are applicable to anyone in the friction zone regardless of the type of decision you face.

Selling a company can be the ultimate achievement of a destination leader. For many entrepreneurs, it is *the* destination. It comes with plenty of benefits: financial rewards, freedom, the ability to work on a bigger stage, new challenges, and growth opportunities. But it's also a major change with complex implications. No matter how hard you try to think through everything, you can't anticipate it all.

I wasn't one of those entrepreneurs who built a company with the goal of selling it. I just wanted to build a great company. But as we built a great company, opportunities came knocking. Even though at first I resisted the overtures, ultimately I felt obligated, to myself and our company, to see who wanted to buy us and what they had to offer. Plus I wasn't sure how long they would keep coming. So I began to entertain thoughts of selling.

Should we shift into another gear or ride at our current pace? Should we continue to grow steadily as an independent midsize agency, or should we join a bigger organization and compete in a global environment? If we sell, who should we sell to? At what price? Under what conditions? When is the timing right to sell? How would we communicate it to our employees? To our clients?

Those were the questions that loomed in my friction zone. I knew I wanted to help the agency get to the next level in ways I didn't think we could do on our own, but I didn't want to do it just anywhere. Nothing was broken. Everything was working well. So the alternative had better be compelling. I met with leaders from several organizations that were interested in acquiring Mitchell Communications, but none felt like the right fit. Then one day I found myself in a corner office on the 16th floor of a building in downtown Manhattan talking to a nearly seven-foot-tall executive at a legendary Japanese mega-agency. Not exactly what I would have predicted, but there I was.

Tim Andree, an executive vice president with Dentsu, has helped lead the company's efforts to successfully expand beyond its Japanese home, first in the United States and later around the world. We first met in Dentsu's New York offices in 2012 to discuss his interest in buying Mitchell, and we sat down there again three years later to reflect on that pivotal time, as well as the challenges of leading in the friction zone.

"We live in such a dynamic environment," Tim told me. "And how to respond to changes and really hit the right gears at the right time is hard. I always start off with a destination in mind, and I end up making wonderful progress, but it isn't always on the exact path that I thought. There were many times I wasn't sure where I was in the friction zone, times when I wasn't sure I was going to catch the right gear."

Tim grew up in Detroit as one of 12 children, and his height and basketball skills earned him college scholarship offers from nearly every major college in the country. He chose Notre Dame over North Carolina, Duke, Kentucky, UCLA, and Michigan. He figured college basketball was the first step toward a lengthy career in the NBA. He would win a few championships, make a bunch of money, buy a big house, marry a wonderful wife, and have a few chip-off-the-old-block children.

In 1983, the Chicago Bulls drafted Tim, but he never saw action in a regular season game.

"I have a wonderful wife and we have lots of children," he said with a laugh, "but none of that other stuff worked out."

Tim played professionally in Europe for a few years and then, at his agent's advice, he went to Japan to play basketball and look for opportunities to use his degree in economics with a global company. He found a day job with Toyota, but initially he was only scheduled to work from 11 A.M. to 1 P.M.

"In other words," he said, "to go to lunch with them and practice English."

Tim started showing up at 7 A.M., looking for ways to prove he wasn't a novelty hire. He quickly worked his way into the business and spent 14 years with Toyota. A few years and a few job changes after that, he made it back to the NBA—but this time he was in charge of the league's global marketing operations.

"I had the full intention of becoming the next commissioner," he said.

Five years later, when he realized he wasn't the heir apparent deputy commissioner, Tim decided it was time to shift gears and found himself in the friction zone. Dentsu, then a 105-year-old marketing and advertising company in Japan, had tried several times to recruit him to help with their efforts to build a presence in the United States. As he took a fresh look at that opportunity, he knew the time was right to say yes. He joined Dentsu in 2006 and helped the company shift from a partnerships and joint venture strategy to a "growth through acquisitions" strategy that focused on building the Dentsu brand on the international stage. This was a bold move by the Dentsu board. The enterprising strategy was led by Dentsu's 11th president, Tatsuyoshi Takashima, and, in the years that followed, by his successor, Tadashi Ishii.

Dentsu was billing $20 billion in 2006, with less than 5 percent of its revenue coming from outside of Japan. Fast-forward 10 years. Due to Dentsu's vision and the leadership of all three men—Takashima, Ishii, and Tim—the company had made multiple acquisitions, Dentsu had more than doubled in size, and 54 percent of its revenues were from outside of Japan. The company now operates in 146 countries, has 47,000 employees, and several world-class agencies as part of the family.

In 2012, however, a few key pieces of the puzzle were still missing, and public relations was a key piece. Tim reached out to me with his interest in Mitchell Communications, and we scheduled a one-hour meeting that lasted two. We talked about how PR was evolving as an industry. We talked about our values and our leadership styles. We talked about our approach to growth. We talked about our beliefs. We talked about our families. We talked about basketball. We talked about motorcycles. In short, we talked about everything but the business aspects of a deal. It was a very different initial conversation from any I had had before.

It was different for Tim, too. The leaders of other agencies he had talked to about an acquisition were interested in discussing how they could "monetize their investment" or how they could "take risk capital off the table" or how they "always deliver" for their shareholders.

"I would look at those guys and say, 'We're not the shareholder,'" Tim said. "'We're looking to be partners with someone.' People couldn't get their head around that. But the human element is really where you end and begin. It comes down to chemistry." Tim made it clear that he wanted Mitchell Communications to be the cornerstone upon which Dentsu would build their PR capability.

Getting the strategy right is crucial too, of course. Tim had a vision and a proposition for me I simply could not refuse. Not only did he want to buy my company, but he wanted me to join his executive team and lead the effort to acquire other public relations firms, building a global PR capability for Dentsu. That was something I hadn't heard from anyone else, and frankly, it appealed to my entrepreneurial spirit. I had built the agency—with a lot of help, of course—and here was a chance for us to build again, but on a global stage. Every other major marketing communications network had added PR years ago and in fact had numerous PR firms in their holdings, all competing fiercely with one another. Tim's vision was fresh and exciting.

It offered a uniquely collaborative environment for us and anyone I could acquire to work with other Dentsu agencies, serving clients together.

When I left the meeting with Tim, I told him the same things I had told every other suitor: "Thank you. I'm flattered. The agency is still not for sale, but I'll think about your offer." In my heart, though, I knew this could be the one.

We continued talking over the next several months, and at Dentsu the potential acquisition of my company soon was referred to internally as "Project Harley." At one point Tim asked me how I would build PR for Dentsu if I came. He asked me to put my thoughts down in writing for him. I decided that would be a good test, and he should see my strategy first.

I sat down on Memorial Day weekend to begin researching and writing in earnest, and within six weeks I had drafted an entire acquisitions plan for a global PR network concept, complete with prospects and growth goals over the next five years. It was a huge undertaking and a bit of a risk to show Tim the playbook. But I also believed it was the lynchpin. Without alignment on this part of the deal, there was no point in continuing the conversation. I felt I was in the friction zone for sure, feeling my way through uncertainty and taking some risks along the way. But I was hoping to find traction at just the right time.

I remember the email from Tim once he had read the plan; he had actually read it several times, he said. He loved it. He had shown it to other top executives in Dentsu, and they also loved it. In fact, they had said, "This is good. Very good." Tim told me Mitchell was the company they wanted to buy, this was the deal they wanted to do, and he hoped I would join the team.

Traction. There it was. I knew it was time to accelerate into it. I was ready to move forward.

I knew Dentsu was the perfect fit for us, but it wasn't only because the strategy and business aspects were right. Just as important, I believed in Tim as a leader and could see that our companies' values aligned.

I remember when I first read Dentsu's 10 guiding principles:

1. Initiate projects on your own instead of waiting for work to be assigned.
2. Take an active role in all your endeavors, not a passive one.
3. Search for large and complex challenges.
4. Welcome difficult assignments. Progress lies in accomplishing difficult work.
5. Once you begin a task, complete it. Never give up.
6. Lead and set an example for your fellow workers.
7. Set goals for yourself to ensure a constant sense of purpose.
8. Move with confidence. It gives your work force and substance.
9. At all times, challenge yourself to think creatively and find new solutions.
10. When confrontation is necessary, don't shy away from it. Confrontation is often necessary to achieve progress.

So much of that matched up beautifully with our five values at Mitchell: trust, open communication, service, results, and commitment. Those values are timeless. I hope they will always be our values. We may live them out in different ways, because our society and our business change, but who we are should always be the same. And I loved that. While on the face of it we seemed so different, there was so much that was really the same between Mitchell and Dentsu.

So over the next several months, I found myself negotiating the details of the deal: the finances, my role moving forward, the timing of the transaction. Fortunately Michael Lasky and Brad Schwartzberg of the Davis & Gilbert law firm helped me understand the value of my firm and assess strategic alternatives and possible buyers during the process. David Wiener of Wiener and Company provided invaluable counsel and guidance throughout the process.

I also had to determine how to communicate with my team and our clients. Telling my executive committee was the first important step. I took them out one by one for a long visit over dinner or in some quiet setting to share the news, starting with Michael, who was a minority stockholder and whom I had kept apprised of all the conversations I'd been having.

Not surprisingly, they all reacted the same way: a bit in shock, not believing what they were hearing, and fearful of what it could mean. But after I painted the entire vision for them: how we were going to position Mitchell for the future, the potential for our people to work with international clients, the opportunity to acquire other agencies and build a new PR capability, the person Tim was and the company Dentsu was, we were all in agreement. The hair was standing on the back of our collective necks, and all five of us knew it was the chance of a lifetime, with a rare match of values that sealed the deal.

It was also incredibly rewarding to share with each of them as well as our leadership team some of the benefits of selling. In fact, right before the deal closed, I hosted a dinner for the leadership team at my home and shared how we planned to use

KEEP (our profit-based bonus initiative for leaders) to ensure they personally benefited financially from the sale. Building the agency was a team effort, and my wealth-sharing philosophy had guided me up until this point to ensure our employees received some personal gain whenever the company did. I wanted to be sure our key leaders knew how much I appreciated their loyalty and service even more so now.

We moved forward as a team to tackle the rest of the communications and organizational planning, carefully and thoughtfully considering how to share the news with our clients, employees, and community at the right time to ensure we had their support. It was a heady time, filled with long hours, countless details, and plenty of anxiety and uncertainty. Consequently, it was most important for me to accelerate into this opportunity with confidence and determination that we were making the right decision, and to help others understand the wisdom and opportunities that were part of the deal.

All leaders face decisions that impact their life and the lives of everyone around them. And any major decision that changes the course of your career and life is filled with uncertainty and complexity.

The unpredictable changes that can come are such a key part of the friction zone that I'll discuss those in greater detail in the next chapter. But there also are some important lessons you can learn as you enter the friction zone that will help you evaluate, make, and execute the biggest decisions of life.

When I reflect on what I learned from Tim and my experience selling Mitchell Communications, the following three key lessons emerged for finding and navigating the friction zone.

Know What Matters Most

As children, we learn to stand, then walk, then ride a bike, and pretty soon we think we have this balance thing down. We grow into adults, however, and we learn there's much more to balance than staying on two feet or two wheels.

You hear a lot these days about work-life balance, and that's important, but right now I'm talking specifically about the balance you need when facing a big decision. That's a type of balance you can only find when you know what matters most to yourself in the context of the world around you, to your family, to your coworkers, to your clients. If you lead a public company, you would include shareholders. In my case, it included Tim and the Dentsu family. It's all the stakeholders in your life.

Tim and I both faced big decisions. He was deciding whether to buy, and I was deciding whether to sell. Yet we were approaching our decisions from the same starting point of understanding what mattered most to us and being certain of the criteria we were using to make that decision.

He knew what he wanted in a company and its leader. He wanted a company that was growing and profitable, had a unique offering, was innovative, and had a proven track record with clients. He wanted a company that Dentsu would complement, so that Dentsu would become better and the company he bought would become better. And on the softer side of the ledger, he wanted to find a match with the chemistry and character of the leadership. He wanted to work with people he could trust to bring a shared vision to life.

I wanted Mitchell Communications to continue growing, but on an international scale as well as through acquisitions.

I wanted the company to expand its influence in ways and in places that probably weren't possible on its own. And I wanted to work with leaders who shared our values and our vision, who appreciated our unique culture and approach to business, and who were willing to take risks to make great things happen.

So it was both strategy and values; the combination of the two mattered most to both of us. That's why our initial conversation—getting to know each other as individuals as well as leaders—and the clear alignment of our organizational values and shared vision for the future were so important to the decision. If either of those things had not been in place, I would not have shifted toward our new reality. I doubt Tim would have either.

Get Your Timing Right

A friend of mine, Scott Boyer, had a successful career in Big Pharma, but he felt compelled to do something disruptive in that industry. When he looked at data analyzing sales and projected sales for drugs, he saw that it always focused on the 10 to 15 wealthiest markets, while a lonely column at the end of the chart—ROW, or rest of world—got almost no attention. In other words, most of the people in the world had little to no access to lifesaving medications simply because they lived in poverty.

Scott talked with his wife about leaving his job to do something more philanthropic, something that would help provide underserved ROW markets with much-needed medications. But they decided the timing wasn't right. They realized they needed to wait until their children had finished college and their personal finances were stronger. When that happened, Scott cofounded One World Pharmaceutical and the ROW Foundation. The for-profit feeds money to the nonprofit to help make treatment for epilepsy available to the 21 million people around the world who could benefit from it but don't have access to it.[3]

When Scott was in the friction zone, he searched for what was important to him but he resisted the temptation to accelerate at the wrong time. As a destination leader, I can tell you that temptation has a strong pull. When I have an idea for attacking a problem, my first instinct is to go for it at full speed. But in leadership, as in motorcycling, you don't always want to accelerate. To navigate the friction zone, we have to learn when to accelerate and when to back off.

Scott and I were talking about the importance of timing when he pointed me to a TED Talk by Idealab founder Bill Gross. My key takeaway from the talk: in a study of more than 200 start-ups, Gross found that timing was the number one factor impacting success or failure, even more important than the idea or the team. The timing of a start-up, or when a product or service was launched, accounted for 42 percent of the difference between success and failure.[4]

Think of it like a curve in the road. You have to navigate it well—look through the turn—to get to your destination. If you accelerate too early, you'll lose control. Too late and you'll lose momentum. You need to go into it at the right speed and accelerate at the right time as you come out of it.

By waiting, Scott not only got his kids through college and saved the money he needed for a start-up, but he also gained additional valuable experience and made connections with the partner who would help define their business and social enterprise model.

Timing was a critical variable in my decision to sell. Looking back, I sold at just the right time because our growth was very strong and our best years were still ahead. I believed we could thrive in a rapidly changing marketplace with the resources of a global partner.

Many entrepreneurs think they should sell when they are ready to retire, they want to move on, or their company is no longer doing as well on its own. Those factors are all negatives for buyers. They want the company that's continuing to grow. They want the force behind the business to stay with the company post-sale, at least for a period of time.

My advice to entrepreneurs: start planning your exit strategy now, even if it's years away. With a clear plan, you'll have a better chance to get the timing right for you, your company, and the new owner if and when the day to sell ever comes.

Find the Traction

The biggest decision of my friction zone experience came when we sold Mitchell to Dentsu at the end of 2012, but Tim was tackling an even bigger one, navigating the $5 billion purchase of Aegis, the London-based media buying firm. This was the other piece of the Dentsu puzzle that was missing. While Tim had been working on it for some time, the deal was not completely finalized until March 2013.

In both cases, timing was critical, because timing is everything when you're trying to find traction. Momentum matters: you must ride it when you have it and be opportunistic when you sense it coming. This is true for anything in life. You have to be ready to go with it when it happens for you, because you can't predict when it will come or when it will go away.

I knew Mitchell had reached the point after 18 years where we needed to make a choice. We could leverage the momentum our rapid growth was giving us to join forces with a larger organization. Or we could settle into our niche and focus on growth we could generate or acquire on our own. The second option would likely take much more time, money, and personal risk to accomplish. It became clear that I had to act soon, if I was going to act, or the opportunity would pass us by.

Sustaining momentum in the friction zone, however, often requires agility and adaptability. Circumstances that impact the decision change, often without warning, and you can lose traction in a hurry. The U.S. Marines have a mantra that symbolizes flexibility, resourcefulness, and quick decision-making: "Improvise, Adapt and Overcome."[5] That mantra applies in the heat of a battle, but it also applies when you're working through the biggest decisions of your career.

Another mantra that's helpful in the friction zone is a Japanese phrase that Tim taught me: *genchi genbutsu*. It means "go and see." Many times in his leadership experience, he followed his instincts to go and see for himself what was happening so he could move things forward or fix what wasn't working.

"This is critical," he said, "particularly at pivotal moments in acquisitions."

In my experiences in the friction zone, there's no substitute for *genchi genbutsu*. You need to get close enough to the situation to see clearly what's going on so you aren't making decisions based on assumptions, and as in Tim's experiences with acquisitions, so you can make sure the right deals happen at the right time.

Genchi genbutsu is about taking action to find out for yourself what the situation is. Taiichi Ohno, the creator of Toyota's production system, was known to take new engineering graduates to the production floor, draw a chalk circle around them, and tell them to stand in the circle and observe at the *gemba* (the place where work is done). If there's a problem on the production floor, he reasoned, it must be understood by going to the production floor.

To get the information you need, sometimes you have to go to the front lines. You have to stay close to truth and reality. You can't assume or rely totally on others for what you need to know yourself.

You can't predict everything that's coming. But if you have the right information, you can be agile enough to deal with change and be ready to ride the momentum when it comes your way. You can sense the point of acceleration where you find the traction and engage the clutch so you can seize the opportunities when they happen.

I'm sometimes asked if I second-guess my decision to sell Mitchell Communications, and that answer is easy: Never. I don't second-guess anything about the deal.

For one thing, that's just not who I am. What good would it do to second-guess a decision when you can't do it over? This isn't golf. There are no Mulligans. You learn from the journey and keep moving toward your destination. More important, I don't second-guess this decision, because I know in my heart it was the right decision, for me and for Mitchell Communications.

Founders eventually must ask themselves, "What is this company beyond me, and how can I ensure its future by making it more about others?" That's the question I faced in the friction zone. Most successful start-ups do well because they embrace a "founder's culture," but they live on only if they embrace a sustainable culture, a culture that's created and lived out by all the people in the organization. It's *their* culture, not just mine. I wanted to position Mitchell Communications to find its own sustainable culture so it could thrive long after I'm gone. Perhaps that's the ultimate gift I could give to our employees, our clients, and our community: for Mitchell to grow and thrive no matter what happened to me.

"I'm sure Mitchell would have been fine just staying on its own," Tim said, "but I'm convinced the agency has a wonderful future ahead of it as part of our organization. I think you stewarded it well, and together with Dentsu I think we can steward Mitchell and all the other agencies we acquire toward something really special. I think together we'll reinvent an industry that has lost its way."

We can do that with Dentsu, but we couldn't have done it on our own. We would have had a future staying just like we were, but we would never have had the opportunity we gained by becoming part of a global company. So although there were risks in selling, the potential for good for so many was greater. That's the thing about the friction zone: it can propel you toward a new destination, but only if you are willing to maneuver through the uncertainty until you find the traction.

The Road Ahead

REVIEW

Life's biggest decisions require you to find and navigate the friction zone so you can find the right traction and momentum to go where you want to go. Accelerating too quickly or too slowly can cause you to miss great opportunities or pursue destinations where you never really wanted to go. These three key lessons have helped me find and navigate the friction zone:

- Know what matters most.
- Get your timing right.
- Find the traction.

REFLECT

- What are the biggest decisions you anticipate you'll be facing in your career or for your business in the next three years?
- Have there been times you needed to "go and see"—when you should have been more in touch with what was happening on the front lines at work? In your personal life?

CHAPTER 11

The Art of the Pivot

One of the things I've noticed through the years is that driven leaders are often restless leaders. It's been true of the driven leaders I've known, including the one I see each morning in the mirror.

We desire change and seek it to ensure forward momentum in our business and in ourselves. We refuse to rest on our laurels and become complacent or lazy. We find that leading others through change is challenging yet incredibly rewarding if indeed the change is significant and positive. So we constantly envision the change that is needed, encourage others to accept and embrace change, and then take them there. We know the end goal is worth whatever they must go through to get there.

But leading through change is hard, even if the change is good. People usually want the outcome, but they resist the process. They want the high-tech new smartphone, but they don't want to learn how to make it work. The outcome is great. The process is uncomfortable.

As if leading change weren't hard enough, we make it harder by failing to communicate well or by failing to think through the impacts of change on people. Or we make it harder if we change just for the sake of change, and not with a clear purpose and goal. Plus, no matter how hard we try, we can't control everything.

That's why a journey mindset matters, because it helps us see change as less about what happens to us and more about how we respond to it. This is what I've come to define as the art of the pivot. It's our ability as leaders to be resilient in spite of change that is difficult:

- To draw deeply from within to fuel our spirit and keep going, no matter how stiff the headwinds
- To understand what we can and can't control, and focus our energy on finding new ways to succeed
- To take detours and use intuition and instincts to make adjustments along the way

The journey becomes far more interesting and rewarding when we approach change with a journey mindset and practice the art of the pivot.

What does that look like? Well, it looks a lot like my friend Jennifer Smith.

Pivoting from Paper

Jennifer is the founder and CEO of Innovative Office Solutions, an office supply company that, as the name suggests, banks its reputation on its ability to innovate. Like every other leader in her industry, she had heard predictions for years that the world soon would become a paperless society.

"People just didn't believe it," she told me.

The change didn't happen overnight, and that made it easy for some to ignore. But it eventually happened, and you'd be hard-pressed to find anyone who doubts it now. Paper and packaging is still a $132 billion industry, but the market for office and writing paper has been steadily declining at a rate of 5 to 7 percent a year since 2004.

That trend wasn't good news to companies in the office supply business. In fact, it was a bigger problem than you might imagine. Companies like Jennifer's (and the big-box office supply retailers she competes against) traditionally counted on paper-related products for at least 50 percent of their revenue.

"We sell 200,000 items that you can order today and get tomorrow, but that one item affected everything we did," Jennifer said. "If you're not using paper, you're not using toner, you're not using envelopes, and you're not using file folders, which means you're not using a file cabinet. So everything we did was affected."

Jennifer faced a challenge every leader experiences at least once, and often multiple times, during the course of their journey: change hits and you have to pivot.

"The indicating signs were there, and I feel we were a little more prepared than most," she said. "A lot of companies in my industry are gone. We've had to reinvent ourselves along the way to stay relevant to our customers."

Jennifer's company not only survived but is still growing, and I believe that's because she understands the art of the pivot. It's in her DNA and it's in the DNA of her company's culture. They are nimble and responsive, so they find ways around life's obstacles and continue toward their destination.

She had built her company around innovation and the core principle that "relationships matter," so the right culture already was in place. Communication was strong. Transparency was in play. Trust was evident. People knew they could try things and not be afraid to fail.

They survived by staying true to their vision of making workplaces more productive and experimenting with new ways to make that happen. It led them to some unexpected places as they went from two product categories to eight.

"Our fastest-growing category is facilities—that is, toilet paper, paper towels, trash can liners," she said. "We've also gotten into the break room, as well as printing, promotional items, and managed print services. We're staying relevant by getting into e-document storage."

Jennifer believes she and her company pivot well for a number of reasons. They stay true to their core principle of valuing relationships, they stress communication and transparency, they intentionally spend time and money on research and new ideas, and she and other leaders anticipate change.

"Leaders who want to grow their business really have to be willing to work on their business and not in it," she said. "You have to embrace that or it's too hard to grow, because with growth comes change."

Bracing for the Inevitable

As Jennifer and her team learned, there are some timeless truths about change: It's inevitable. It's good. It's bad. It's messy. Sometimes it's all of these things at the same time. This was brought home again to me just recently when I was preparing for a speaking engagement. I surveyed a select group of about 50 seasoned leaders, nearly three-quarters of whom had been in a leadership role for more than 15 years.

When I asked about the biggest change they'd been through in the past three years, more than half cited organizational changes: a company reorganization, the establishing of a new partnership or dissolving of a partnership, mergers and acquisitions, or other changes in ownership. Another 30 percent had experienced change in their roles and responsibilities. These leaders all saw the positives as well as the negatives. Change offers interesting challenges. It allows you to develop new skills. It leads to innovation and creativity. It sharpens your competitive edge. It helps you grow profitability.

As I looked at the responses more closely, I saw two distinct types of change: the kind you initiate and the kind that comes at you unexpectedly. It's that second kind—the kind most of us like the least—that's the hardest and requires you to pivot as a leader.

It's tough, the leaders in the survey told me, because you don't have time to prepare. You don't always have the information or support you need, and that leads to confusion, distraction, and frustration. You're less certain about the outcome. Then you come upon the boulder in the road . . . the ultimate obstacle: loss of control, which forces you to find a new way forward.

Leaders like to drive change, not be driven by change. But as the survey confirmed, we often don't have that luxury. That's a lesson I learned firsthand, and it's how I personally discovered how to master the art of the pivot.

My Personal Pivot

You might think my biggest experience with change came in 2009 when our company was pushing through the recession and beginning to grow so dramatically, or late in 2012 when we sold the company, but that's not the case. Sure, those times involved change. Lots of change. The change wasn't always easy, and in fact, at times it was very hard. But each time we were on a path to an amazing destination that by and large I drove and controlled. For the most part, I figured out a plan for dealing with the changes we faced.

Immediately after we sold the agency, 2013 was a terrific year with Dentsu as our parent company. We were integrating into a global network, meeting and working with people from different countries, winning new clients, hiring new staff, opening new offices in Chicago and New York. I handed off the day-to-day responsibilities of running the agency to our executive vice president, Sarah Clark, whom I promoted to president. I retained my CEO title and took on an additional title as CEO of the Dentsu Public Relations Network. Then I set about tackling my new responsibilities to build it.

The top priority for this new role was to identify and acquire public relations firms to join our network. I studied dozens of agencies and met with a short list of prospects. I also went on an internal listening tour, meeting with more than 80 leaders throughout Dentsu and the company's previously acquired agencies globally to ensure I had a good grasp of what we needed in PR capabilities for the future. By fall I was in negotiations to buy three different agencies and having serious conversations with several more. I also found myself in some new places: I was the only female leader sitting on Dentsu Network's international operating committee, and I was traveling more often than not, including to some fascinating destinations such as Tokyo, London, Paris, and Toronto. I was in overdrive, working hard but knowing I was laying the groundwork for hitting some significant goals in the years to come. It was an exciting time, both for me as a leader and for our company. We were all growing and thriving.

The bigger challenge came a year later when Dentsu bought Aegis Group, a London-based agency that at the time had 12,000 employees operating in 80 countries. The two large companies formed a new global organization called Dentsu Aegis Network. It was a great fit. Aegis complemented Dentsu, filling in several gaps to make the overall organization far stronger. But as with any merger, it brought changes: changes in workflow, reporting structure, processes, expectations, culture, priorities, performance goals, strategies . . . change, change, change. Because of all of these unexpected changes, the plans we had made also needed to change.

Our focus was always on serving our clients, but successfully integrating with and getting to know our new organization became the next most important priority. I had to shift my acquisition work from overdrive into neutral. All my negotiations needed to stop until we could reevaluate our strategy for a very new global organization. It was an exciting time because of the greater potential, but a challenging time because of the unexpected shift.

Frankly, it was as if I had been racing across the desert with an oasis in sight only to suddenly find myself on a motorcycle I had never ridden before. Then I was on a steep mountain with switchback curves. I had mapped a course, but it no longer applied. The landmarks I expected were no longer relevant. Everything was different, except, of course, that I was still moving so fast that I hardly had time to read the signs.

I remember thinking to myself, "We've been through so much change already, how much more change is there going to be?" We had just been through year one with Dentsu, now we were going through another year one with Dentsu Aegis Network. I couldn't have foreseen that we would have to go through two integrations and that much of my acquisition work in 2013 would be for naught because of the change in strategy. I'm a destination leader, and I was eager to make progress toward our goals.

The more I thought about it, the more I knew I needed to course-correct and fast. I spent a considerable amount of quiet time reflecting on all that had happened and thinking about how to move forward from here. Personally, I wanted to dig as deeply as I could to find strength from within and my way back to a journey that mattered. First, I got some much-needed perspective. I reminded myself of my personal blessings: family, friends, health, and financial security. And in the new network, we were still the flagship PR agency with a green field in front of us.

Next, I fast-forwarded in my mind to some point in the future and wondered how I would look back on this challenging phase in my life. I didn't like what I saw: someone who was spending time and energy feeling frustrated and uncertain. I didn't want those things to define this pivotal time. I reminded myself that I had always been a fighter, especially through the many years of building the agency in less than ideal circumstances. I reminded myself that it's not what happens to you in life that matters; what matters is what you *do about it*. I reminded myself that success isn't promised; we have to work for it and stay the course to find it, and sometimes it's not easy to find even then. I also reminded myself that success is not the ultimate victory, it's the "try" that counts the most.

I emerged from this time of introspection with renewed hope, courage, and commitment. I found myself again, but it was a stronger, better self, a wiser and more determined leader. I knew I needed to share my fresh perspectives with my closest leaders, and I did so by hijacking our next executive committee meeting. As the team walked into my office, I told them we're scrapping the agenda to work through five important questions. I had a flipchart on an easel in my office and turned over the top page to reveal the list:

1. What is our reality?
2. What can we control and can't we control?
3. What do we want?
4. How will we get there?
5. What do each of you want?

I started by apologizing to them for being frustrated, and I made a declaration: "Despite all the change happening around us and to us, we will succeed," I said. "I know we can do it, and I'll do whatever it takes to help us get there." We must have talked for more than three hours, working through all the questions and really pushing ourselves to think less about the challenges and more about the opportunities. Then I went around to each person individually and said, "I want to win. I believe we can win. And I want you here with me when we do.

Are you in?" After much laughter, many tears, and renewed commitments, we were indeed all in, and never more so.

Throughout the rest of the year, we faced even more change such as some unexpected client budget cuts due to downturns in their business, but we never gave up and maintained a clear focus on success even while we tried to find our way on this new path. We ended up hitting many of our goals as an agency, and I rolled up my sleeves to develop a fresh acquisition strategy that would make the most of our new network's enhanced value proposition.

As we rallied and rose to the challenges, it began paying even greater dividends. We established relationships with our new sister agencies—there were 20 different brands in the United States alone—and began collaborating with them to serve existing clients and win additional ones. In fact, our agency is often cited as the most effective collaborator among the U.S. agencies in the network, and much of the credit goes to our new business team and client service leaders who demonstrated a spirit of reciprocity and partnership from the get-go.

Our revenue continued to grow, and our profitability remained above the industry average. We added new capabilities and services, doubled the size of our New York office, refreshed our brand, and continued attracting top talent across the agency to help serve clients in an exceptional manner. Our tenacious leadership team is largely responsible for these achievements. They demonstrated great determination and drive to win even while we were adapting to and integrating with a new parent company. I also hit the acquisition trail with a new strategy that was focused on building a global PR brand rather than a PR network, and I began talking with many prospects about our new vision.

Today we feel more optimistic than ever about the agency's future. We're on a path to a different destination than I imagined when deciding to sell the agency in 2012, but we believe it offers just as many opportunities for us to succeed, and we are determined to make the most of them. Together, we learned the art of the pivot.

Leading Through Change

So how do you deal with change? Not just the change you initiate or participate in creating, but the unexpected wave of change that hits you blindside and causes you to stumble or lose your balance altogether?

I'm a big fan of John Kotter's seminal work *Leading Change*. I was fortunate to hear him lecture during the executive training program I took part in at Harvard Business School, and we spent an entire day working through his eight-step process for change management.

Here's the short version: Establish a sense of urgency. Build the guiding team. Get the vision right. Communicate for buy-in. Empower action. Create short-term wins. Don't let up. And make it stick. This is textbook change management, and it works. But it's hard to pull out a textbook when unexpected change comes, and it will come. So before you can check the textbook and practice great change management, you have to pivot and deal with the new as it's happening right in front of you.

So here's my art of the pivot checklist for managing change in real time.

Accept Reality

You can't make change during change unless you first accept what is happening. It doesn't help to blame others or blame yourself. None of that is a productive use of your energy. Think about what is so and then ask, "What's next? What can we do about it now?"

Remember my friend Jennifer? She was an early adapter to the fact that the world was using fewer paper-related office products. Accepting that reality before her competitors helped her stay in front of the pack.

Break Glass, Pull Handle

There are times you need to be bold and move swiftly. You have to make a decision. You need to move with confidence, and you need to make something happen, because everybody is looking to you in that moment. It's easy to lead when the wind is at your back, but it's altogether different when you have to take the helm in the storm and guide the ship. Yet that's when you are needed the most. That's when you must break the glass, pull the handle, and say, "This is where we're going and how we're going to get there."

Tell the Story

It's up to you as the leader to help others around you understand the need for change and the plan for moving through it. This is where your communication skills really come into play. You must become an effective storyteller, providing the context for change, showing your vision for where the organization will go from here, and underscoring the sense of urgency. You must share that story over and over again, and continue communicating throughout the change as progress is made.

Don't Turn Back

Leading during change isn't easy, and you have to tolerate conflict and personal anxiety to get through it. This can be challenging for leaders who are very relational like I am, because change can stress relationships. You might feel you've let someone down or that he or she let you down. Or people don't agree with you. Or you feel the anxiety that comes with being responsible for the livelihood of the people who work for you. It's tough. But you can tolerate more than you think you can, and you have to push through the conflict and anxiety. As Winston Churchill said, "If you're going through hell, keep going." There isn't any way to turn back, and it's a waste of time and energy to second-guess your decisions. You'll feel like you're walking through the fire when you are in these moments of personal anxiety. So keep your eyes focused on where you want to end up, and be the one with the clear head and the calm heart who can keep things moving forward.

Expect the Unexpected

This seems so obvious, yet we seldom do it. When we're in the middle of life, we're focused on what's in front of us or on the plans we're making for the future. We're focused on our destination and how to get there. Then the road shifts beneath our wheels. By looking through the turn, we're anticipating change and we're more adaptable, nimble, and responsive.

This takes focused effort. Regularly ask "What if?" questions that help you spot potential change sooner rather than later. What if our customers' needs fundamentally change and they no longer want what we offer? What if there is a change in our company's top leadership that directly impacts me? What if a new technology disrupts the way we do business?

When we were motorcycling in the Alps, my husband would stop at times on the road and look down the mountain to see what we might encounter over the next few miles. He wasn't just riding into the unknown. He was learning as much as possible about that unknown and never forgetting that something unexpected might pop up around the next turn.

Keep Something in the Reserve Tank

There's a common myth that motorcycles have a reserve gas tank, but there's only the one tank that sits between you and the handlebars. This tank does get smaller at the bottom where there's an intake straw, and when the fuel drops below this point, your motorcycle sputters and comes to a stop. But by turning the petcock valve, you can access the gas that's still in the tank and travel another 20 or 30 miles. So it acts as a reserve.

I love that analogy because when we're dealing with change, we all need access to a reserve of internal strength and determination that allows us to power through the critical moments when most others will quit. This is exactly what I was looking for during my time of reflection and regrouping. This is the time our team needs us most. But in order to have that reserve when you need it, you must build it up in advance by fortifying your emotional capacity, clarifying your sense of purpose, and strengthening your desire to succeed. You must also take care of yourself physically, not becoming so run-down or out of shape that you lose the stamina and clear-mindedness to face change.

Another effective strategy is to engage your leadership team regularly in problem-solving and build a cohesive group that is willing and able to tackle anything together. This should bolster your confidence knowing that the burden doesn't rest just with you but with a strong team that can carry great weight together if needed. This is something I've always tried to do, and Jennifer has found this strategy to be very effective in her leadership experience, too.

"If you are willing as a leader to share when you are worried about something and you take it to your team, it helps diffuse that fear," she said. "You pull your team together and you work on it. If you have the right support staff, or a leadership group you're in, or your board, you can turn to them, too. If you aren't harboring everything, it's so much easier to deal with those fears. There are things that keep me up at night, but the fear part of it hasn't been horrendous because I haven't harbored it all."

Let Change Change You for the Better

The greatest lesson I've learned—and greatest benefit—is that change changes you. You are never the same person again. You'll have a different view on life and leadership. It will make you bitter or it can make you better.

Earning your own self-respect is what matters most of all. That means being able to look back on any challenge and know you did your best. You can't control many of the outcomes in life, but you can control your attitude and your effort. When you are in a state of unexpected change, it's difficult to give your best. But that's when it really counts.

So it's important to be a learning leader. Be coachable; you don't have to know it all. In fact, you can't know it all, so learn as you go.

The challenge of change is an absolute necessity of a leader's journey. It is the refiner's fire that forges in us stronger character, more profound wisdom, deeper empathy, and greater resiliency. That's exactly the kind of leader I want to be after change. How about you?

Coping with Change

When I find myself struggling to cope with the challenges of change—whether it is change I'm leading or change that's hitting me unexpectedly—I find it easy to lose focus and lose faith. When it happens these days, I immediately think of my friend Tommy Van Zandt.

Tommy built a successful career with Phillips Petroleum before starting a second career in commercial real estate. He cofounded Sage Partners in 2005 and quickly helped build it into one of the most successful and respected full-service real estate firms in Arkansas.

But in 2009, everything changed for Tommy. One of the worst ice storms in the state's history hit that winter, causing damage all across the region. In the aftermath, Tommy climbed a ladder to clear broken trees and large limbs off his property. He accidently fell, and a severe spinal cord injury due to the impact left him paralyzed from the neck down.

Tommy spent much of the next two years in and out of hospitals, and today he still battles the challenges of fatigue, confinement to a wheelchair, and the need for specialized breathing equipment. But he has returned to work. He's in the game and he's making a difference. He has become a picture of resiliency and heart in the face of tragedy.

He doesn't speak often in public, but when he does, Tommy presents a message of hope and healing for others. You would be surprised, in fact, how little he says about his accident or his condition or his struggles. He talks about building relationships, leading with integrity, and making a difference in the lives of others.

He could complain and be bitter about the change that happened to him, and who would blame him? But Tommy reminds me that no matter what happens, we need to stay in the game and keep fighting for the win. Tommy embodies this so well, not only in how he lives his life, but also with the words he shares. Tommy shared a famous quote with a group of young leaders he was speaking to recently, and it beautifully captures the essence of dealing with change:

> It is not the critic who counts; not the man who points out how the strong man stumbles, or where the doer of deeds could have done them better. The credit belongs to the man who is actually in the arena, whose face is marred by dust and sweat and blood; who strives valiantly; who errs, who comes short again and again, because there is no effort without error and shortcoming; but who does actually strive to do the deeds; who knows great enthusiasms, the great devotions;

who spends himself in a worthy cause; who at the best knows in the end the triumph of high achievement, and who at the worst, if he fails, at least fails while daring greatly, so that his place shall never be with those cold and timid souls who neither know victory nor defeat.

—THEODORE ROOSEVELT

Thank you, Tommy (and of course Teddy Roosevelt), for reminding us all who are striving to be destination leaders with a journey mindset and searching for wisdom on leading through change. This we can carry with us: no matter what you face, get in and stay in the arena. That's where all the action is anyway. May we never be timid souls.

The Road Ahead

REVIEW

There are times in life when we grab the bull by the horns and force change to happen. It might not be easy, but we're creating a change for the better. At other times, the bull tosses us to the ground and begins to charge, horns down and eyes filled with fury. Time to master the art of the pivot.

Here's my art of the pivot checklist:

- Accept reality.
- Break glass, pull handle.
- Tell the story.
- Don't turn back.
- Expect the unexpected.
- Keep something in the reserve tank.
- Let change change you for the better.

REFLECT

- When have you experienced unexpected change in your life? How did you deal with it well, and in what ways could you have dealt with it better?
- Do you have the internal strength, emotional capacity, and sense of purpose that will sustain you during challenging times ahead?
- What are you doing to maintain your physical well-being now so you can perform at your best when you are put to the test?

PART III

Enjoying the Ride

CHAPTER 12

Awakening

Sometimes the most important lessons in life are painfully slow to sink in. That's been the case for me, at least, especially when it comes to merging a journey mindset with destination leadership. Thankfully, with the help of friends, family, and God's grace, life continues to provide opportunities for us to "get it."

When Raye and I moved to Arkansas in 1995, I began to understand a little bit about the importance of enjoying the ride. Life presented a detour, so I scrapped the map and kept going. But in all transparency, I didn't take the lesson fully to heart. Instead, I simply rerouted with the same hard-core focus on my new destinations.

I've had other aha moments through the years, but the real wake-up call came nearly a decade later. Even then it took more than two years to fully pull me out of my slumber, and ironically, it all started because I couldn't sleep.

As Raye would tell you, I seldom struggle to fall asleep. My head hits the pillow, and I'm out. In 2006, however, I found myself caught in a disturbing trend. Each morning I would wake up around 2:30 or 3 A.M. This wasn't just roll-over-and-go-back-to-sleep awake, it was wide-eyed-can't-stay-still awake. I would fight it, of course, but inevitably I would get up, work on the computer, and watch for the sun to rise before it was time to get the kids ready for school.

I love to soak in a beautiful sunrise as much as anyone, but even that gets old after a few weeks, especially when it means you have to start each day with only a few hours of sleep. So finally I went to see my good friend and internist, Dr. John Furlow. Surely, I thought, I had some physical ailment he could write me a prescription for or wave a magic wand to fix. He listened patiently for a few minutes as I described my issue, and then he offered this advice.

"Elise, you're healthy as a horse," he said. "I know you are a driven person and you usually are going and blowing all the time. But something is keeping you awake at night, and you need to get to the bottom of it, or you're not going to get a good night's sleep for a long time to come."

Well, the problem was, I didn't want to get to the bottom of it. I knew what was bothering me, but I didn't want to face it. What was waking me up at night, and keeping me up at night, was a simple question burning in my brain that would never go away: "Is this all there is?"

The question unnerved me for two reasons. One, I was afraid of what I might discover if I actually answered it. Two, I felt ashamed to be asking this question in the first place. I had so many blessings—a great family, a successful career and company, great friends. Life was good. How could I possibly want for anything else?

It was a chilling time, because for one of the first times in my life I began to doubt who I was and the value of my destinations. As those doubts gained a foothold, I began to second-guess some of my decisions. For instance, not long before I began enduring my sleepless nights, I had been offered two extraordinary job opportunities. These were high-level leadership roles with exciting organizations, but I ended up turning both down to stay with my own business. It was the right decision in both cases, but in the months that followed, my mind began to torture me with second-guessing. The devil on my shoulder kept whispering in my ear: "Good work. You didn't just pass up one dream job—you passed up two."

It hit me that I might always be doing exactly what I was already doing, and for some unknown reason, what I was doing suddenly didn't feel like it was enough. So I woke up in the middle of the night asking myself over and over, "Is this all there is?"

"I Can't Run Any Faster . . ."

Chariots of Fire debuted in 1981 and quickly became one of my favorite movies. It won four Academy Awards, including Best Picture and Best Screenplay, for the artful way it captured the real stories of two very different British athletes who competed and won Gold Medals in the 1924 Olympics.

One of them, Harold Abrahams, was an intense runner, a man on a mission and with a passion to win at all costs. He was driven, disciplined, and determined, and in the end, he won an Olympic gold medal in the 100-meter dash. As the movie unfolds, however, you get a picture of a man who finds no joy in his training or in the competition itself. He appears so driven by his pursuit of the goal that all he cared about was winning.

There is a defining moment in the movie when Abrahams loses a race to Eric Liddell, his arch rival and the other athlete featured in the movie. Abrahams' girlfriend, Sybil, attempts to console him in his moment of defeat. Her message is essentially this: "You'll get him next time." But she doesn't realize something much deeper has paralyzed Abrahams, and it comes out in desperation as he confesses to her: "I don't think I can run any faster." In other words, he admits in that moment that he is afraid he may never be any more than he already is. Think about the fear those words can cause in the heart of a leader. Not a good feeling.

I believe all leaders, and especially all destination-focused leaders, face crucial questions at some point, if not multiple points, during their careers: *Is this all there is? Is this all I'll ever be? What if I can't get any better? What's the point of my work? What's the purpose of my life?*

It was particularly paralyzing for me because I got up every day driven to get one step closer to a goal. Achievement defined my value. It had become my identity. It had become who I was. Confronting my deepest fear—that this is all there is and I can't run any faster—was more than I could bear, even when my doctor prescribed it as the cure for my sleepless nights.

Instead of getting better, my problem only grew worse until one day I showed up for a client presentation without my shoes.

I had left the house in a rush, as usual, and I was certain my shoes were in the car. Of course, I didn't take the time to check, and so off I went to my meeting—in bare feet. This was my life, unfortunately: nonstop, frantic, and sometimes shoeless.

When my friends heard this story, they could have laughed it off as just another crazy day in the fast-paced life of their fast-moving friend. Instead, they saw it for the warning sign that it was, and they recommended I take some time off. They knew these types of moments were starting to define my life; they weren't just exceptions to an otherwise normal existence. So on the heels of my shoeless meeting, Raye and I took off on our motorcycling trip to Europe.

I fell in love with riding while on that trip, and I took it up when we returned, but it still took time for me to actually slow down and change my mindset. A little less than two years later, in fact, I went to lunch with two leaders in my company and spent most of our time verbally lashing out in frustration over the performance of our team. Frankly, we weren't hitting the marks of excellence I expected, and I feared it might cost us one of our largest and most influential clients. I ranted about our team's inability to do the level of work I wanted to see from them, and it didn't make for a pleasant lunch, at least not for my colleagues.

Unfortunately, this was not an uncommon scene. I found myself constantly frustrated with others: no one seemed to be getting it right, no one was giving it their all like they should (or like I would). In truth, no matter how hard those around me worked and the level of excellence they delivered, it was never enough for me. I had fallen into a black hole of unrealistic expectations and adopted a demanding demeanor that only made others feel they could never hope to keep up.

When I got home that night, Raye asked me to sit with him at our kitchen table and talk. He said someone from work had called out of concern for me. In fact, he and the kids were concerned, as well. Everyone—everyone but me—saw the pattern. They all loved me, but they didn't like what they saw in the person I had become. Raye lovingly told me in no uncertain terms that something had to change. I had to get help.

And I finally did.

Getting off the Speedway

Every fall, teams of professional drivers converge on Le Mans, France, for a motorcycle race. That's not unusual, of course. Le Mans is well-known for its races—automobiles, motorcycles, and just about anything else that moves. And motorcyclists regularly race on all sorts of tracks all over the world. But for this race, the Bol d'Or, teams of three drivers each circle the track continuously for 24 consecutive hours in an event that tests the endurance of both the riders and their equipment. It's fast, furious, and . . . monotonous.

It might seem insane, or at least boring, to spend so much time driving around the same track, even during racing conditions. But that was my life in 2006. I was spending day after day, week after week, month after month, and year after year driving around the same track in pursuit of a finish line and a trophy. I had become *all* about the destination.

With the help of people like Raye, Dr. Furlow, my closest friends, and my colleagues at work, I began making a number of changes, some of which I believe can provide help for any leader who faces, or wants to avoid, life on a never-ending Bol d'Or.

It was during some intense soul-searching after Raye's kitchen-table intervention that I finally answered the question that haunted me. First, I admitted that destination leadership had so consumed me that my purpose in life had become defined by my achievements. Then I came to realize that my problem wasn't that I was pursuing unworthy destinations; the problem was that I had missed the journey along the way. In my relentless pursuit of the destination, the journey no longer mattered.

I decided that if I could make the journey matter more, then perhaps I could find meaning and purpose for the path I was on—and satisfaction and contentment from my work and in my life. So how do you give more meaning and purpose to the journey?

In management and consulting circles, you sometimes hear the phrase "start, stop, continue" as a tool for evaluating personal or team challenges. So that's what I did. I identified the things I needed to start doing, the things I needed to stop doing, and the things I needed to continue doing (but typically needed to make a higher priority). Here are a few lessons I learned.

1. Sometimes You Must Release the Destination

I've always considered myself a lifelong learner, but it was usually with a purpose of reaching a destination. I wanted to learn more so I could achieve more. I've come to realize I'll always be on a journey, always learning, and always figuring it out, and that there are times when there's no destination required for us to reap the joys life can offer. I realized that you can't work all the time and that you have to learn to experience the joys of rest.

Rest is an interesting concept for a hyperactive person like myself. It can involve stopping and not moving—and I've always struggled to do that—but there also are active forms of rest.

If you'd asked me a few years ago what my hobbies were, I would have told you that I didn't have any, because I didn't have any free time. I knew that needed to change, if for no other reason than because I wanted to be an attractive, engaging person for my husband. He didn't want to be married to someone who was defined by only her work.

So I found hobbies that relate to a journey mindset. I learned to ride a motorcycle and began riding alongside Raye. I took up running, one of the joys of my youth, and completed my first half marathon in 2009. I'll never forget telling Raye after I crossed the finish line, almost screaming, "I've never felt so alive!" I also learned to fly-fish, a sport that requires skill, patience, and perspective. I fell in love with it on my first outing. I didn't catch a single fish, but I learned that "catching fish is incidental to the experience," and you can say with great confidence to anyone who asks: "The fishing was good; it was the catching that wasn't so great."

These things are meant to be experienced, not accomplished. You might ride toward a destination or run toward a finish line or cast for trout, but it's the experience, not the results, that bring the real joy. Life and work can be that way, too. J. J. van der Leeuw, a Dutch author who spent much of his life exploring philosophical and theological ideas, got it right when he said, "The mystery of life is not a problem to be solved; it is a reality to be experienced."

2. Find Your Dashboard Moments

It sounds a bit cliché to say we should "enjoy the moment," but like many clichés, it's rooted in truth. The reality is, many of us find this cliché easier to dismiss than to live.

I found one of the ways leaders can enjoy the journey the most is to look first at our families. There was a time when Raye and I both spent so much time at work that we found ourselves spending brief periods of "quality time" with our kids. Then we realized it was more important to spend lots of "sloppy quantity time" with them. Ironically, the more time we spent with them, the more we found quality in our time together.

For seven years my daughter was on both school and competitive cheerleading teams, and we frequently traveled around the country for competitions. I drove her to most of these events, and in the beginning I would take my laptop and phone and work whenever I could. But the more I started putting it away, the more I noticed that she began to open up with me. On late-night trips home with just the glow of the dashboard light around us, she began to talk to me about life, love, salvation, self-esteem, you name it. Anything worth talking about, we began to talk about it. I had similar moments with our son, Jackson, when traveling for baseball and basketball tournaments. I call these dashboard conversations. Had I not been paying close enough attention, I easily would have missed the small voice from the backseat that said, "Mom, can I ask you a question . . ."

For many leaders, it's not always easy to "be there" and listen to our family when they call out to us, because work never stops throwing challenging issues at us that we need to think through and solve. But if we don't learn to be present in the moment with our family, we'll look up one day and find that we lost step with them long ago.

3. Work to Live

I've heard it said that most people in the world "live to work," but people in Colorado "work to live." For most of my first 25 years in the workforce, I thought that philosophy to be worthless. Now I find it essential.

Henry David Thoreau faced this dilemma and left his home to find out what life was all about by living on a pond in rural Massachusetts. You may recognize this quote from Thoreau: "I went into the woods because I wanted to live deliberately. I wanted to live deep and suck out all the marrow of life . . . to put to rout all that was not life; and not, when I came to die, discover that I had not lived." There is pure joy in truly savoring life itself, regardless of whether we're at work or at play.

We find joy at work by loving what we do and doing it to the best of our ability. There is satisfaction from a hard day of work, even if the end goal was not accomplished. I once thought that if I could not cross everything off my to-do list and accomplish what I had set out to get done, then I had wasted the day. Then I learned to find joy in whatever came my way. Even if it prevented me from a timely arrival at some pre-established destination, I realized that I had:

- Helped an employee
- Solved an unexpected problem
- Addressed a client's immediate and unplanned need

I realized I had found joy in my work. I had worked to live.

We see this lesson vividly brought to life by the other runner in *Chariots of Fire*. Eric Liddell is portrayed as the exact opposite of Harold Abrahams. Liddell loved to run and he experienced every moment as if it was a gift from God, which, of course, it was. Liddell was one of the favorites to win the 100-meter dash, but he had dropped out of that event because one of the heats was on a Sunday. For Liddell, Sunday was the Sabbath, a day of rest, and therefore he wouldn't compete. To the dismay of many of his countrymen, including several high-ranking politicians and royalty, he instead ran as a huge underdog in the longer 200- and 400-meter events. In the scene that shows the 400-meter finals, Liddell has an expression of pure joy on his face as he presses his way to Olympic gold.[1]

Chariots of Fire shows us two different runners who both win the prize, but by using two very different approaches to how they ran their races. I can tell you with all assurance that while I used to be Harold Abrahams, with every day that passes, I am trying much more to run my race like Eric Liddell.

That doesn't mean destinations aren't important. It means I have a better understanding of what matters most to me and of the importance of investing in other parts of life and taking care of myself. It means I realized that a leader can succeed as a mother and wife, while still succeeding as a CEO. I discovered a leader can have it all, just not all at the same time. And that's more than enough.

The Last Crop in Fallsville

By the fall of 2009, I could confidently say I had made the turn toward a journey mindset that brought balance to my destination style of leadership. I wasn't there—I'm still not there—but I was on a better course. So when Labor Day weekend rolled around that September, I had no problem rolling away from my work and enjoying a ride on my bike.

Raye and I met his father, a good friend, and another couple just as the sun came up for a beat-the-heat ride through the Ozark Mountains of Northwest Arkansas. Our self-appointed navigator was born and raised in these hills, so we fell in line behind his Harley as we started out from Fayetteville. The general plan—after a pit stop for biscuits and gravy in Huntsville—was a ride through Newton County, a sparsely populated county with winding highways that are quite popular among cyclists.

The first hour or two of our ride took us through small towns, some beautiful rural areas with tree-covered hillsides, sprawling farms, and tiny churches with inspiring signs like, "We use duct tape to fix everything. God used nails."

By midmorning, we decided to stop at a bend in the road called Fallsville. The small gravel lot had a lone white building with a single glass door, and three old-timey gas pumps. No credit card swiping here. You're gonna have to go in, which was our intention anyway. We needed a stretch.

We discovered the only available restroom didn't require a key—outhouses apparently don't need that much protection. As we laughed about this, I noticed not far from us an old pickup sitting under a tree. An overall-clad gentleman was perched on the edge of the passenger's seat with the door standing open.

Sprawling around the truck were piles of plump green-striped watermelons. I didn't need a cutting to know they'd been picked at the height of their juicy glory. I decided to wander over for a visit, and Gentleman Gene, as I think of him now, broke into a smile at the prospect of a buyer approaching.

"How's business," I asked, curious if he had, or if he really expected, to sell any melons that day.

"Picking up," he said. "They're beauties, and better than anything you've ever tasted."

Certainly a convincing argument, especially on a hot summer day.

"You raise pretty melons," I agreed as I looked them over.

He got out of his seat and leaned on the side of the truck. The entire bed was filled with dozens more melons.

"I'm just trying to get whatever I can for them today," he went on. "They're not mine. They're my neighbor's."

Gene, as it turned out, was a proud farmer who just couldn't stand the thought of letting perfectly good watermelons rot in the field. So he had driven to his neighbor's house that morning and convinced him to let him load up his truck and come to the gas station to try to find a home for as many as possible.

"Why wouldn't your neighbor bring them himself," I asked. Seemed like a nice but strange thing to do, hauling off your neighbor's bounty. Was his neighbor lazy, tired of eating melons, tired of giving them away?

His answer caught me off guard. "He's just not up to it this year. He's got cancer pretty bad. He'll never make another harvest. This is his last crop."

A new appreciation for the melons flooded over me, and their natural beauty just shone. Gorgeous shades of green, smooth round skin, plump centers. Just the way they were at rest on top of each other looked as if someone had carefully placed each one in a certain spot to catch the morning's light through the trees. I began taking pictures of them.

Gentleman Gene went on to tell me how his neighbor had lived off the land his whole life, reaping what he sowed and scraping together enough along the way to feed and clothe 14 children. An experienced chef after a fashion, he had taught all the women in the area to make homemade sorghum molasses. Gene grinned, "I think the most he ever made in a year was $1,200. Some of it from his melons." No doubt.

Our conversation was interrupted by the sound of motorcycle engines. I looked past him to our group. They were putting helmets on and folding maps. Time to get going again. I thanked Gene for his story and apologized for not being able to take some melons with me.

"They don't make saddle bags big enough for melons," I said. "But I want you to do something for me." He leaned forward. "Please tell your neighbor you met someone today who thought these were the most beautiful melons she had ever seen. That she took pictures of them and promised to share their beauty with others."

He laughed. "That will make him smile, and I haven't seen him smile in a long time."

As we rode away, I thought about fall, but not with the welcome anticipation I'd felt that morning. Harvest is a time of plenty but it's also a time of endings. I never used to think about things winding down in life; I was always too wound up. But of course there is a time of harvest that comes for us all. The real question is what are we harvesting?

Gentleman Gene had done his neighbor a favor, but he'd done one for me, too. It may have been a last crop, but it won't be one that's forgotten.

So that haunting question, how do I answer it now? I have realized that this isn't all there is; there's a lot more out there for me to experience. I believe that's true for any leader who wants to achieve great things while connecting to a purpose that doesn't define them by their achievements.

For the first time, I knew I didn't have to know how it all ends. I became content to leave the destination unknown and determined to enjoy the journey along the way.

The Road Ahead

REVIEW

I try to keep an open mind about most things, but I was especially hardheaded when it came to facing my fears as a leader. Facing your fears, however, is the key to merging destination leadership with a journey philosophy. If you get nothing else from this book, get this: you will never fully enjoy the journey toward any destination until you put your fears in their place and put your priorities in order. Here are the three most important things you can do to get past your sleepless nights:

1. Realize there are times when you must release the destination.
2. Find your dashboard moments.
3. Work to live rather than living to work.

REFLECT

- On a scale of 1 to 10, how much meaning and purpose are you finding in your journey? (1 is none, 10 is more than you know what to do with.)
- What makes you doubt yourself as a leader?
- What's your answer to the question, "Is this all there is?"

CHAPTER 13

Journey Toward Significance

I've discovered that as we mature and more fully embrace a journey mindset, we also find more and more opportunities to use our unique gifts, broaden our impact, and move to a higher calling of leadership. This is the journey toward significance.

It doesn't happen when we reach a certain age or have a certain title or find ourselves in a certain income bracket. It begins when we allow it to begin by letting ourselves embrace a journey mindset that redefines our understanding of success to include significance. It happens when we make it happen and take actions based on that mindset.

This higher call of leadership is really about stewardship. That's because it's not about how much we have, but what we do with what we have. It's achieving significance in our leadership experience by using what we've learned and earned to benefit others, not just ourselves.

The opportunities to change the lives of others and "pay it forward" are the most valuable fruits of leadership success.

They provide significance to the journey and a destination worth pursuing. It's the ultimate payoff of being a destination leader with a journey mindset.

When I made the decision to go from a success-building destination philosophy to a wealth-sharing journey mindset, my life changed dramatically for the good. I could see the impact. My success was not just for myself or the people around me. It was much broader. Everything in my life became more rewarding.

When You Have the Opportunity to Do Good

I've always tried to be a generous person, someone who supported worthy causes and invested in the lives of others. But a series of events beginning in 2010 reshaped my understanding of what it really means to be a "giver." I discovered a deeper joy, as well as the practical benefits that came, when I freely gave away my time, my money, and even work in light of my passions and in support of the greater good. I didn't really realize how much giving could change me until I unexpectedly found myself simply saying yes to my heart and making a significant donation to my alma mater.

This story begins on Facebook of all places. For many years I had made an annual donation to my alma mater, Abilene Christian University (ACU), to fund a scholarship I had established for top students majoring in public relations (PR). I was messaging on Facebook with Dr. Cheryl Bacon, the chair of the Department of Journalism and Mass Communication, about the scholarship. Our friendship went back to my days as a student when she was one of my instructors, so our messages weren't all business. But at the end, she thanked me for the scholarship donation and noted that they were about to begin construction on a new space for their student-run advertising and PR agency.

The students had been running the agency for about two years. They worked on real projects with real clients who paid real money. But they needed a bigger, more professional office with the right equipment. This was the first time I'd heard about it, and I was blown away by the concept of the agency. Since I had built an agency of my own, I had an immediate passion for the project, and the idea of giving students real-world agency experience before they graduated was simply powerful.

I asked for more details, and as Cheryl told me about the project, I asked where they were on funding. Turns out, they were still significantly short of the amount they needed to get it across the finish line. She also told me how much it would take to get it done.

When I read that number, two thoughts popped up. First, *that's a lot of money.* And second, *I actually have that much money. I've never given that much to something all at one time, but in this case I could.* I found myself wrestling with a simple question: What should I do? ACU had done so much for me and had helped paint the picture of the kind of leader I wanted to be in life. Perhaps this would be just a small down-payment on a much larger debt of gratitude I was eager to repay.

I sent her another message: "Cheryl: I'd like to give you the money you need."

Needless to say, she was thrilled and grateful. We laughed and we cried, tears of joy for both of us. It felt good to have helped Cheryl and the students, and I trusted that many good things would come as a result.

But honestly, I didn't think much about it after that, other than writing the check. Then a month or so later, Cheryl wrote to say how excited the students were about the project. In addition to renovating the classroom into office space, she said they were renovating the name. (The "ACU Student-Run Ad/PR Agency" wasn't cutting it.)

After researching agencies at other schools, they decided to name it after two people. First, they picked Don Morris, the president of the university from 1940 to 1969. He had given money to build the Morris Center, the building that housed the agency. Also, his grandson had been a student in the PR program and had died of cancer in his forties. So naming it after Dr. Morris made perfect sense. They also wanted to honor someone special who had supported the agency.

"The students have met and want to name it Morris & Mitchell," Cheryl told me via Facebook, "but only with your permission. We would like to be able to tell people that we chose Mitchell because you are an alum who models what we want our students to be professionally, and because you have helped get the agency off the ground with your gift. May we have your permission?"

I didn't know what to say. I was no equal to Don Morris, and I hadn't anticipated the students wanting to do this. The thought of it made me a bit uncomfortable. It is one thing to have your name on the door of an agency you actually run, but it is wholly another to have your name associated with something you had little to do with its success. Yet the more I thought about it, I was honored by their intentions and happy to lend my name if that would help the agency and the students. I began to look forward to the opening of the new office that fall as a proud alum and now a proud giver.

In October I traveled to Abilene for the grand opening, along with a number of special events Cheryl and the team had planned. It had been many years since I'd been back on campus, and I thoroughly enjoyed a trip down memory lane. I walked all over the campus. I went to my old dorm. I sat in "my" chapel seat. Everything the university had done to set me up for success and shape me as a person flooded over me like a waterfall.

I toured the agency and saw a first-class, contemporary facility. I met and spoke with the many talented students who were involved. To top it all off, the students surprised me at the ribbon-cutting with a motorcycle helmet customized with the Morris & Mitchell logo.

The entire weekend was fantastic, and many of the students tagged me in photos on Facebook. When I arrived at the Mitchell Communications Group office on Monday, I was greeted with plenty of questions about the pictures. They knew I had been to visit my alma mater, but I hadn't mentioned anything about the gift or the student-run agency.

As I explained all that had transpired over the past few months, I relived the impact of the gift. It felt like a way to thank the school that had given me so much, personally, spiritually, and professionally. I really found myself at that school. I could never repay the school for all it did to help me get started in life. But it gave me such pleasure to be able to contribute financially and see how the students might benefit from the gift.

One of my dear friends and a key leader at the agency, Blake Woolsey, sat down in my office, looked at me, and said, "You're different. Just the way you talk about this gift. The glow on your face. You're different."

And I realized she was right. I was different. The experience of giving at that level had changed me.

"It's priceless," I told her. "I wish I could bottle this—how good it feels to give and know you're going to impact lives."

"You simply found that intersection between your passion and the opportunity to give," she said. "That's magic."

In the years that followed, that gift led to a string of additional financial gifts, but also in a relationship between our agency and Morris & Mitchell. We worked on projects together. Their students interned with us. I began visiting ACU more regularly and dropping in for informal chats and mentoring time with students. In 2012, I used some of the proceeds I personally received from the sale of the agency to permanently endow Morris & Mitchell's operations, establish a new video production agency called 39 West, and fund several other new projects. One of those projects was a diversity program that helped the department maintain its prestigious national accreditation. Both 39 West and the diversity program were also partly in honor of our creative services group at Mitchell Communications and our Big Break diversity initiative.

The lesson in this is simple: when you have the opportunity to do good for others and you feel moved by the spirit, you should do it. If I had kept that money, I could have invested it. I could have spent it on something for myself. But that would never have meant as much to me as the joy of helping these students. Don't second-guess the desire to give. When you are compelled by an overwhelming conviction to act, do it. Then stand back and watch all the good that will happen, giving you a sense of satisfaction that is worth far more than anything you could receive had you kept the money for yourself.

Igniting the Gift of Giving

The more I felt the stirrings of gratitude and satisfaction that came from making that initial gift to Abilene Christian, the more I wanted others to feel what I felt. Specifically, I wanted people at Mitchell Communications to have the opportunity to feel that way.

So one day shortly after my conversation with Blake, I walked into the office of our COO Michael Clark.

"I have this crazy idea," I said. "I want our people to have that experience, but on our time and dime. What if we gave them money and an afternoon off to go into the community and do random acts of kindness? Is that possible?"

"Sure it is," he said. "Absolutely, we can do it."

We quickly put a plan in place for how we would make it happen, scheduled an afternoon to get everyone together, broke them into teams, and handed each team a stack of cash.

"Come back with nothing except a story of giving," we told them. "Who did you help, and how did it impact you as a giver?"

They went out and found people in need: children in schools, elderly hospital patients, victims from a recent tornado, and mothers struggling to pay for their laundry or their groceries. They came back with stories that filled our office with laughter and tears.

So from my experience with Abilene Christian, something else was born: We named it "Ignite," and it's an annual event that lives as tangible proof of our values and our desire to give back to our communities. It's probably my favorite day of the year at the agency.

Ironically, after I gave the larger gift to ACU, Cheryl was looking for a unique way to say thank you. She read about Ignite, and thanked me by creating a program now known as "Ready, Set, Give." Teams of students in the journalism and mass communications department are given money to give away in the Abilene community in the same fashion as Ignite. She had no idea Ignite had been born from my giving experience with ACU. Somehow the pleasure of giving had come full circle.

Giving All the Good Stuff Away

Giving time, money, and energy to the things you're passionate about often isn't easy. But once you do, it leaves such a powerful feeling of significance that you never want to stop.

Some leaders hold tightly to everything they earn in life and sadly, never experience this joy. But it's not just money to which they cling. The other thing that's hard to pry from a leader's hands, even a leader who is generous with money, is control. But giving this away also provides amazing returns, for a leader and for an organization.

During our second big stage of growth at Mitchell, our team had grown to around 70 people. I knew I had to step away from some of the "craftsman" work I was still doing, but I wasn't exactly sure what stepping away looked like or how to do it. I had just established the executive committee, and I knew there was an opportunity to empower these senior leaders with some of the roles and responsibilities I had been doing for years—if I could bring myself to do it. A phrase I'd heard somewhere kept echoing in my mind . . . "Focus on what only you can do and give the rest away."

I wrote it on the flipchart in my office and stared at it for inspiration. I thought if I looked at it long enough, somehow it would convince me that I should do it, and maybe tell me how. It didn't speak to me. But it did inspire me to think through what that message really meant and what it would look like to live it out.

A few days later, Kate Andersen, our vice president of Creative Services at the time, noticed the phrase on the flipchart and asked me what it meant.

"Well, let me ask you a question first," I said. "What do you think is the most operative word in that sentence? What one word is most critical?"

She looked at it, reading silently to herself: *Focus on what only you can do and give the rest away.*

"I don't know," she said after a few seconds. "Maybe *you* or *focus.*"

"Nope," I said. "The operative word is *only.* If you take the word *only* out, what does it say? Focus on what you can do and give the rest of it away. So what *can* you do in the business? Well, if you ask me that question, I'll say everything."

For most entrepreneurial leaders, that's the case. They can do everything, because they have, by choice or necessity, done everything. There was a time when I had done everything. I handled the billing, managed the payroll, swept the floors, and locked the doors. I had won and managed every single client we worked with in the early years. And part of me still wanted to be involved in everything.

Then I added, "Well, I'm still trying to commit to this. I want to jump in and do all these things that I know I can do. I want to come over there and help you run Creative. Should I be doing that? Absolutely not."

The larger an organization grows, the more it needs and depends on specialists rather than generalists. As a leader, you may know how to do lots of things, but that doesn't mean you need to regularly do them all. So what things should you do? The things *only* you can do and that bring the greatest value to the business.

When you become a specialist, you have a defined role. There are tasks that only your role or that only you in that role can and should do. Those things are unique to you, your talents, your capabilities, your expertise, your knowledge, your experience, and your credentials. But you can't do those things and everything else you've always done. The same is true for leaders.

"So what do you give away?" Kate said.

"All of the good stuff," I said with a smile. "Power, authority, credit, recognition, relationships, information, resources, knowledge, you name it. And that's the challenge. That's why so many leaders hit the wall at this point and can't push through. They can't give away the good stuff."

Making the conscious commitment to focus on what only I could do and give the rest away seemed good in theory. But I also thought I'd committed to a decision that would send me to the unemployment line. I remember sitting at my desk and thinking, "Well, I don't have a job anymore; I just gave my job away. All these things that I was so busy doing, that I was great at, and that made me feel so good about myself—I just gave it all away. There's nothing terribly meaningful left for me to do."

So I pulled out a notepad and pen and started jotting things down—things only I could do—not because I was the only person qualified but because they were unique to my role as CEO or because I was, indeed, uniquely qualified.

Surprisingly, it didn't take long for my list to grow.

I had never really written a detailed growth plan for the company. I was always too busy managing the growth we had. *Maybe I could develop a three-year growth plan*, I thought. *Managing and reacting to growth is not a growth plan.* So I decided to flesh out some future opportunities we could proactively pursue.

I also thought about our finances. I was involved in all things related to money for the company, whether it was coming in or going out, of course, but I didn't have a deep understanding of true finance. I wasn't a classically trained business management professional. I didn't have an MBA. I would look at the numbers when they came through, and I would ask our CPA and controller questions from time to time. But I was never really very strategic about finance, because I was limited in my knowledge. So I decided to make that year my "year of finance." I committed to learning everything I could about finance so that I could make more informed and strategic decisions for the company.

When you begin to make a list of the things that only you can do by design and by definition of your role and your abilities, it becomes very empowering. You realize there are certain assets you bring to the organization that are incredibly valuable.

By the end of the week I had 14 items on my list. I remember having the following realization, when I looked at the list: "This is the job of a CEO. It's the job of the coach, not the quarterback." When I was willing to give up the ball and become the coach, the new list of what I needed to work on was a mile long, with the potential to make a far greater impact on our company.

I realized this was a normal part of our transition. It was part of my growth professionally and our growth as a company. I knew the time had come to lift my head from the desk, look through the turn to see what was coming, and figure out where we were going and how we could get there. I needed to work more *on the business* and less *in the business*. I needed to release many of my other responsibilities to the leaders around me.

This was huge for me. I think it's one of the most important moments of growth any leader can go through. It requires a leap of faith, because it challenges you to give up a lot of the things you're good at. But it allows you to develop your talents and abilities as a leader, as well as the leaders around you. You take yourself to that mystical "next level" of leadership because you are willing to become a learner again and take on new tasks, goals, and responsibilities.

When you give up all the good stuff, the payoff is twofold. Your team gets better and you get new, really good stuff. You become a master craftsman at different crafts. You discover, as I did, that you're much more valuable to the organization when you become a passionate expert in the role you're most needed. All the stuff you gave away becomes a valuable gift to the people around you.

Seeing Others as Whole Persons

When I talk about finding significance in your journey, the obvious examples revolve around giving away things that it takes a great deal of time to earn. Most of us aren't born wealthy. We have to earn money so we can give it away. Most of us aren't born into the role of a high-level leader. We have to earn that mantle so we can give it away.

But the heart of what I'm really talking about when it comes to significance truly has less to do with money and titles than it has to do with serving others. Because no matter where we are or how much money we have, we always can find ways to serve the needs of others. The only thing you need to share your wealth is to share yourself.

One of the most powerful examples I know of is found in the story of my friends Kent and Amber Brantly. Kent is a doctor and Amber is a nurse, both very respected professions in the U.S. culture. You might expect such a couple to earn a good income, live in a nice home, drive nice cars, send their kids to nice schools, and there's nothing inherently wrong with any of that. But Kent and Amber's sense of calling—first, to serve God, and, second, to serve other people—led them to jobs with a clinic in Liberia. When the Ebola epidemic broke out in Western Africa, Kent and Amber found themselves right in the middle of it.

Kent and Amber are ACU grads, so we met through alumni-related events, and I visited with them one evening while they were home in Fort Worth. I knew they had something to teach me about giving yourself away in service to others even when the circumstances are tough.

"Residency was tough," Amber said, "but living and working in Liberia and through an Ebola epidemic was tougher."

It became even tougher in 2014 when Kent contracted the disease. In fact, he was the first American to return to the

United States for treatment of Ebola. His survival story is the topic of *Called for Life,* the book he and Amber wrote. His commitment to helping in the fight against the disease was a reason *Time* magazine included him as one of its Persons of the Year for 2014.

As we talked that evening, I quickly discovered that the sense of significance they had about their work is what allowed them to experience joy and peace in the most challenging of situations.

"When I was laying in my bed dying of Ebola," Kent told me, "I had incredible peace because I knew we were living out God's calling on our lives. So even though I thought I was going to die, Amber didn't hear me saying that I wasn't anxious or afraid. I sure was. But I was okay, and I don't know that there's anything more rewarding than that. That's not what you would normally think of as rewarding. But for the significance of what you're doing to bring you peace even in the face of death, I think that's been the most rewarding thing about the life we've chosen so far."

Kent and Amber approach their work as something more than just "doing a job." Even if you're a doctor or a nurse, you can do your job without really caring for someone's holistic needs. You can make diagnoses, prescribe treatments and medications, or give shots without knowing or caring much about what else a person needs to feel whole. As leaders in corporate environments, we can do the same. It's all too easy to get laser-focused on budgets or strategies or goals or deadlines and forget that we have an opportunity to care more deeply about the needs of those around us.

Kent shared a story that really speaks to what it looks like to care for the whole person when we're at work.

Two women, Lusu and her adult daughter, Josephine, had become sick with Ebola while caring for Lusu's other daughter, who had contracted the Ebola virus while working as a nurse. That daughter had died, and Lusu and Josephine were brought to the Brantlys' clinic for care. Both of the women were very sick.

One night Josephine began crying out for help. It took Kent and his team about 30 minutes to suit up so they could safely enter the treatment unit. By the time they got there, it was too late. Josephine had died.

"Her mother was just a few feet away and had watched the whole thing happen," Kent said. "That night was one of the most difficult of my life."

Ebola is most contagious right after a victim has died. But Kent decided he needed to act immediately to remove Josephine's body so Lusu would not have to endure the additional anguish of having her daughter right in front of her. Even though he wore protective gear, Kent was nervous as he and his team took care of Josephine's body while also considering the heartache of a mother who now had lost two daughters to the disease and was dying from it herself.

"After that night, Lusu became very solemn and quiet for the next day or so," Kent said. "She had just become stoic and she was requiring total care. She couldn't feed herself; she couldn't get out of bed to go to the bathroom. But you know, I had the advantage of not just seeing her illness. I was able to see her as a whole person, because I was there witnessing the tragedy that was unfolding in her life. I knew that I was not just feeding a lady who couldn't feed herself, but I was sitting there holding the hand of a woman who had just lost two of her daughters and was dying."

As he held her hand, Kent began thinking about the song "Today O" by Nigerian singer/songwriter Wale Adenuga. It was a powerful song he and the staff often sang during their daily devotional meetings.

"You could always feel the emotion as they sang this song," he said. "And often I would have to stop singing because I would think about the lives these people have lived and the tragedy and the horror that they had lived through with 20 years of war and conflict."

As Kent told me the story, he closed his eyes and began softly singing, just as he had sung that day at Lusu's bedside.

Today O I lift up my voice in praise
For I know that you are always there for me
Almighty God, You're my all in all
No matter what I face, when troubles come my way
I will praise You Lord

When he sang those words to the despondent Lusu, she squeezed his hand and gave an affirming nod, saying so much more than words could have.

"It was like that song was the prayer she needed but didn't have the words for," Kent said. "And for the next two days or so, she really perked up. She started talking to the nurses. Her condition improved. Not much, but a little bit. She came out of that stoic shell and connected with a couple of the nurses. After about two days, she died. But I think what we were able to do for her was meaningful. Even though the disease took her life, I think we were able to treat her with dignity and respect and compassion even in the midst of her tragedy. I think it was meaningful."

I love that lesson so much, and as Kent recounted it to me, I was deeply moved by the way in which he as a leader had cared for someone far beyond the transactional requirements of his job. In fact, it struck me how he had done something truly magnificent when no one was looking. In one of the darkest places on Earth—in the heart of the Ebola epidemic in rural Africa—Kent had led not only with determination and commitment, but with true passion to help others in a quiet and selfless way. Simply because it's the right thing to do, and he had an opportunity to do it.

It reminds me that as leaders we can always shine a light in the world and in the workplace when a clear purpose for what we do drives us. I may not be on a mission field like the Brantlys. Nor can I save anybody's life, like my husband, who also is a doctor. But I can still do something that brings light to people right where I am in the workplace.

Kent's story encourages me to go beyond treating employees, clients, and others in the business world from merely a transactional point of view and see them instead as whole people. I can stop in the hallway and serve a fellow employee or just tell them I care about him or her. I can let clients know I am thinking about them when I know they are hurting. I can have a sharing mentality with other business leaders and strive to assist those who need my help. We can't see everything, but sometimes we can see more than we realize if we look close enough. Caring for those around us and having a positive impact on their lives is another powerful way we as leaders can find significance in the journey.

Doing Good . . . Today

Kent is often asked by others and by himself why he's still alive. Why was he able to survive a deadly disease that has taken the lives of more than 10,000 people around the world?

"The answer I keep coming back to is that I can never come up with a satisfactory answer to *why*," he said. "But I will always have to answer another question: so what now? You can spend all day philosophizing about why and where this is headed, but you've got to do something with where you are right now."

Not long after I spoke with Kent and Amber, I was part of a discussion panel at a conference in Chicago. The moderator asked each of us to give some parting advice to the emerging leaders in the audience, so I talked about the importance of finding significance in the journey. After the session, a young man thanked me for what I'd said and then pressed for something more.

"How do I find significance?" he said.

I was a little surprised by the question, but I thought for a moment and then answered him.

"I'm not sure how *you* find it," I said. "But here's how I found it. I've learned what I'm passionate about. It starts with my faith, and it encompasses things I truly love, such as leadership and helping others lead at their best, writing and speaking, supporting my alma mater. I've found ways to work these things into my life outside of the workplace to help impact others for good and in the process bring greater joy to my own journey. What are you passionate about that you can devote yourself to and that would change you and those around you for good? What do you love that gets you out of bed every day?"

He gave it some thought and said, "I am sure I can think of many things. When should I start?"

"Today is always the best day to start something new," I told him. "You can begin your journey toward significance by simply taking that first step now."

As the young man walked away, I felt encouraged by the conversation and determined to take my own advice. "Today" is an empowering thought for sure. Today I can start finding deeper purpose in my work. Today I can take a new path on my leadership journey. Today I can do something magnificent for someone else. Today is the day!

Don't wait until you've got plenty of extra time and energy, or until your savings account is flush or your investments are rolling. Don't wait until you've retired from the workforce. Don't wait on anything. When you have the opportunity to do good for others, do it. When you can give good stuff away, give it. When you have the chance to love the whole person, love that person.

Every decision you make, every action you take—they all add up to the story of your life. You are writing the chapters every day.

Don't delay. Start today.

The Road Ahead

REVIEW

Taking advantage of opportunities to use your unique gifts and broaden your impact is a high calling of leadership that moves your journey toward significance.

1. When you are compelled to do something good for others, just do it.
2. Focus on what only you can do, and give the rest of it away.
3. Care for the whole person.

REFLECT

- Is there a donation, regardless of the size, you could make to a worthy cause that would allow you to find the magical intersection of your passion and the opportunity to give? What organization might you give to?
- What "good stuff" can you give away to one or two others on your team who would love the opportunity to receive something of great value from you?
- Think of someone you know through work who would benefit if you treated him or her as a whole person—someone you could tell that you are thinking of him or her as that person is going through a difficult time, or someone you could offer to assist in a meaningful way.

CHAPTER 14

There Awaits

"We're the real 'wild hogs,'" they said in unison, huge smiles spreading across their faces, one of them flashing the peace sign just in time for me to snap a picture.

We had stopped at a small gas station in Bodega Bay overlooking the harbor, about an hour north of Sausalito on Pacific Coast Highway 1. The cool breezes from the water were a welcome contrast to the summer heat and humidity back home.

Raye and I were on our first real adventure of the empty-nest era. Just two months earlier, we had dropped off our second (and youngest) child at the US Naval Academy in Annapolis for the start of plebe summer and freshman year. Jackson had accepted an offer to play football for the Midshipmen. Raye and I were still pretty raw from the letting go—not to mention the actual moment of good-bye. It had been a similarly bittersweet experience when Mackenzie left for Lipscomb University in Nashville three years earlier. As hard as we had worked to get all of us ready for their launches in life, leaving them on the doorstep of college turned out to be a lot tougher than we had thought.

That is why we had planned this trip. Raye and I needed something to look forward to, and what better way to regroup and recharge than another motorcycle adventure? It had always done the trick before.

So we drove up from the Central Coast with Kirk Specht, a friend we'd met in 2008 on a motorcycle tour with Edelweiss Bike Travel of the Pyrenees, the majestic range of mountains that form the natural border between France and Spain. He loaned us a bike, a BMW RT1200, and we fell in right behind him. We set out for points north, planning to stay as close to the coast as possible and looping back again in a few days just in time to catch our flight home. Where we ended up didn't really matter. We just wanted to ride and somewhere along the way find our way back to ourselves.

As we pulled into the gas station, we immediately saw them: two older bikers, probably in their seventies, dressed head to toe in black leather, and astride pretty souped-up sport bikes—Ducati Testastretta 11s to be exact. They were filling up for the road ahead. As is often done in the biker community, we wandered over to admire their bikes and ask about their travels.

"Where are you headed?" we asked.

"Anywhere the road takes us," they responded with no hesitation. "We ride all the time now—every week. No place in particular. Both of us are retired, and we've downsized. We don't need much these days, except of course our bikes."

And good weather, which is pretty plentiful along the California coast.

We could tell by listening that both had enjoyed some measure of success in their careers. Now they'd made a conscious decision to shelve a lot of the trappings of achievement and focus their resources on things that mattered more to them, like their friendship and the journey.

"How often do you ride?" they asked.

The three of us answered practically in sync: "Not enough," and we all laughed somewhat wistfully.

Kirk had been in the same season of life as us, busy building an orthodontic practice for the previous 20 years and being a dad to two children, both now grown.

"It's never enough, no matter how much you ride," added Kirk.

I agreed. I loved my life, but the season we'd been in was filled with our children's activities and the building of businesses. Lately I'd been putting in the miles on airplanes instead of motorcycles. It was important to focus on these things while we had the opportunity. But it left me longing for more rides to anywhere the road would take me.

Now the seasons were changing. I'd arrived at a destination—gotten to another "there." This destination was filled with satisfaction, a lot, in fact:

- The satisfaction of seeing my children happy, healthy, and continuing on their own journey. We would always cheer them on, but theirs was a new path, one that would take them where they want to go.
- The satisfaction of seeing my company soar to new heights and our team experience growth and learning like never before. This was the satisfaction of stretching myself as a leader and seeing how change was changing me for the better.
- The satisfaction of celebrating more than 25 years of marriage to the same wonderful guy, and appreciating how rare that is anymore.
- The satisfaction of having friends for a lifetime who have loved me, and I them, come what may.

It was all a great destination. A great "there" to arrive at. But somehow, not enough. Even still, after all the journey mind-set I'd been trying to infuse into my thinking over the past eight years or so, I was still hungry.

I stood at the gas station and snapped a picture of the two wild hogs. They were pretty cute in their own way, hopping onto their bikes, waving to us as they left. The picture of care-free. I thought I should want what they had, perhaps 10 or 20 years from now: to ride into the sunset and never look back. Isn't that what we're supposed to work for?

Perhaps. But honestly, I've never wanted more out of life than I do now. Spending my days riding a lonely highway is the furthest thought from my mind. Not that Raye and I won't find the open road on many occasions between now and then; we've already planned our next bike trip, which will be in Norway. But I've got plans—big ones. And miles to go before I sleep. That's the nature of a destination leader. We are wired to set our sights on the horizon and head over the next hillside, no matter how beautiful it is here.

The difference now is that I won't miss the scenery along the way. Whether I'm on a beautiful coastal highway, pulling myself out of a ditch somewhere along a rocky road, or working through a leadership challenge with my team, I'm not going to miss a single minute of this magnificent journey called life.

Maybe in that way I have found what I was looking for after all, and what the wild hogs have found as well but with many more years to appreciate it: joy in the journey.

And no matter where the road leads, if I keep my eyes focused on where I'm going, I'm certain I will end up there. After all, "there" awaits.

The Road Ahead

REVIEW

Thanks for joining me on this journey. So what's your game plan? How are you going to change your life to explore the roads and lead through the turn? Use this final Road Ahead section to reflect on actions that will propel you toward your next destination while still allowing you to enjoy your journey. Think deeply about these questions, and use your answers as a starting point for a plan of action.

These aren't questions you can put off, because time won't wait on you. "There" awaits.

REFLECT

- Where do you want to end up, and is what you're doing getting you there? If not, what do you need to change?
- Are you enjoying the journey? If not, where do you need to change your focus?
- How can you leave a leadership legacy not only of business excellence, but more important, of changed lives and a better world?

Appendix

Recognition

Elise Mitchell and Mitchell Communications Group have been recognized on numerous occasions for their accomplishments, including the following:

- 2016 Global Power List, *PRWeek*
- 2016 Power List, *Arkansas Business Journal*
- 2016 Woman of the Year in Business, Arkansas Women's Foundation
- 2015 Outstanding Alumna of the Year, Abilene Christian University
- 2014 Cannes PR Lions Jury member
- 2014 Co-Chair, PRSA International Conference
- 2014 Midsize Agency of the Year finalist, *PRWeek*
- 2014 Two Sabre awards, *The Holmes Report*
- 2013 Eight Telly awards
- 2013 Diversity Champion, Diversity Distinction in PR Awards, PR Council and *PRWeek*
- 2013 Agency PR Professional of the Year, *PRWeek*
- 2013 Top 50 Power Players in PR, *PRWeek*
- 2013 Top 10 Fastest-Growing PR Firm, *The Holmes Report* global rankings

- 2012 Five APEX awards, PRSA Northwest Arkansas Chapter
- 2012 Award of Excellence for Public Service, PRSA
- 2012 Best Large Business, Fayetteville Chamber of Commerce
- 2012 Five Silver ADDY awards, Northwest Arkansas Chapter
- 2012 Inc. 500/5,000 Fastest-Growing Companies in America, *Inc. Magazine*
- 2012 Small Agency of the Year, *The Holmes Report*
- 2012 "50 Fastest-Growing Women-Owned/Led Companies in North America," Women Presidents' Organization/ American Express OPEN
- 2012 Enterprising Woman of the Year, *Enterprising Women*
- 2012 Most Influential Women, *Talk Business Quarterly*
- 2011 Outstanding Entrepreneur, Women of Excellence Awards, National Association for Female Executives
- 2011 "50 Fastest Growing Women-Owned/Led Companies in North America," Women Presidents' Organization/ American Express OPEN
- 2011 Inc. 500/5,000 Fastest-Growing Companies, *Inc. Magazine*
- 2011 Best Minority/Women-Owned Business, Fayetteville Chamber of Commerce
- 2011 Two APEX awards, PRSA Northwest Arkansas Chapter
- 2011 One Gold Addy, Northwest Arkansas Chapter
- 2011 One Silver Addy, Northwest Arkansas Chapter
- 2011 Two APEX awards, PRSA Northwest Arkansas Chapter

- 2011 Small PR Agency of the Year, *PRWeek*
- 2011 PR Agency of the Year, Honorable Mention, *PRWeek*
- 2011 Dorothy Brothers Scholarship Recipient, Women's Business Enterprise National Council
- 2010 Business of the Year, *Arkansas Business*
- 2010 Business Executive of the Year, Finalist, *Arkansas Business*
- 2010 *PRWeek* Boutique Agency of the Year, Finalist, *PRWeek*
- 2010 Four APEX awards, PRSA Northwest Arkansas Chapter
- 2010 One Silver ADDY, Northwest Arkansas Chapter
- 2009 "10 Most Powerful Women in Arkansas," *About You* magazine
- 2009 Lillie Knox Growth Award, Women's Business Council of the Southwest
- 2009 Customer Service of the Year Award, Walmart Financial Services
- 2009 Three APEX awards, PRSA Northwest Arkansas Chapter
- 2009 Two Gold ADDY awards, Northwest Arkansas Chapter
- 2009 Two Silver ADDY awards, Northwest Arkansas Chapter
- 2008 Regional Volunteer of the Year, Women's Business Council of the Southwest
- 2008 Three APEX awards, PRSA Northwest Arkansas Chapter
- 2007 "All-Decade Class" *Northwest Arkansas Business Journal* 40 Under 40

- 2007 Seven APEX awards, PRSA Northwest Arkansas Chapter
- 2003 Athena award for leadership and community service, Fayetteville Chamber of Commerce
- 2002 Business Executive of the Year, *Northwest Arkansas Business Journal*
- 2002 40 Under 40, *Northwest Arkansas Business Journal*
- 2002 Public Relations Professional of the Year, PRSA Northwest Arkansas Chapter
- 1993 Public Relations Professional of the Year, PRSA Memphis Chapter

Notes

CHAPTER 2

1. Northwest Arkansas Council, "Researchers Put Northwest Arkansas 3rd in Future Economic Growth," June 20, 2014, http://www.nwacouncil.org/news/2014/jun/20/researchers-puts -northwest-arkansas-3rd-future-eco/.
2. "Best Places to Live," *US News & World Report,* accessed March 10, 2016, http://realestate.usnews.com/places/rankings-best-places -to-live.
3. Helen Handfield-Jones, "How Executives Grow," *The McKinsey Quarterly* (Winter 2000), http://www.questia.com/library/journal /1G1-60014740/how-executives-grow.

CHAPTER 4

1. http://www.bls.gov/opub/mlr/1985/11/art3full.pdf.
2. This blog offers some nice insights into the numbers on the freelance economy: Lydia Dishman, "Is the Freelance Economy Not Growing as Much as We Thought?" (December 15, 2015), http://www.fastcompany.com/3054620/the-future-of-work/is-the -freelance-economy-not-growing-as-much-as-we-thought.
3. John Wooden, *They Call Me Coach* (New York: McGraw-Hill Education, 2003).
4. Diane Coutu, "Leadership Lessons from Abraham Lincoln," *Harvard Business Review* (April 2009), https://hbr.org/2009/04/ leadership-lessons-from-abraham-lincoln.
5. Welch referenced the "boundaryless company" as a goal for GE in its 1990 annual report. I learned of it later in this article: Larry Hirschhorn and Thomas Gilmore, "The New Boundaries of the 'Boundaryless' Company," *Harvard Business Review* (May-June 1992), https://hbr.org/1992/05/the-new-boundaries-of-the -boundaryless-company.
6. Sanjeev Agrawal, "How Companies Can Attract the Best College Talent," *Harvard Business Review* (March 17, 2014), https://hbr .org/2014/03/how-companies-can-attract-the-best-college-talent/.

CHAPTER 6

1. "Intercensal Estimates," U.S. Census Bureau, accessed August 14, 2016, https://www.census.gov/popest/data/intercensal/.
2. Teresa M. Amabile and Steven J. Kramer, "The Power of Small Wins," *Harvard Business Review* (May 1, 2011), https://hbr.org/product/the-power-of-small-wins/an/R1105C-PDF-ENG?Ntt=%22progress%20principle%22.
3. Check out a video about Ignite at https://youtu.be/_VuZfeUFmDY.

CHAPTER 7

1. Avi Dan, "Kodak Failed by Asking the Wrong Marketing Question," *Forbes*, January 23, 2012, http://www.forbes.com/sites/avidan/2012/01/23/kodak-failed-by-asking-the-wrong-marketing-question/#bd355f07dd7b.
2. Carl Honoré, "In Praise of Slow Thinking," updated May 25, 2011, http://www.huffingtonpost.com/carl-honore/in-praise-of-slow-thinkin_b_331843.html.
3. Warren Berger, "The Secret Phrase Top Innovators Use," *Harvard Business Review*, September 17, 2012, https://hbr.org/2012/09/the-secret-phrase-top-innovato.
4. Here's a link to more detail on this model: http://www.designcouncil.org.uk/sites/default/files/asset/document/ElevenLessons_Design_Council%20(2).pdf.
5. Brian Solis, "Why Businesses Back Innovation Centers," Crunch Network, October 5, 2015, https://techcrunch.com/2015/10/05/why-businesses-back-innovation-centers/?utm_content=buffer47e49&utm_medium=social&utm_source=twitter.com&utm_campaign=buffer.
6. David Maister, "Innovations about Innovating," Passion, People and Principles, post 233, November 6, 2006, davidmaister.com/innovations-about-innovating/.

CHAPTER 8

1. Here's a link to a rider on a snow-packed mountain, but Google can help you find any number of additional versions: www.youtube.com/watch?v=iT3g-faK460.
2. https://www.ideo.com/about/.
3. Fitzgerald, F. Scott, "The Crack-Up," *Esquire*, February 1936, http://www.esquire.com/news-politics/a4310/the-crack-up/.

CHAPTER 9

1. A list of the awards we won is available in the Appendix.
2. A video of my testimony is available at www.youtube.com/watch?v=4RZp0Q5w6PY.

3. www.americanexpress.com/us/small-business/openforum/ keywords/state-of-women-owned-businesses-report/ and http:// www.womenable.com/content/userfiles/2016_State_of_Women -Owned_Businesses_Executive_Report.pdf.

4. Mitchell, Elise, "Broadening Your Network: How Strong Stakeholder Relationships Can Work for You," PR Council, August 8, 2012, prcouncil.net/voice/2012/broadening-your-network-how -strong-stakeholder-relationships-can-work-for-you.

5. Mitchell, Elise, "Mrs. Mitchell Goes to Washington," *PRWeek*, August 10, 2012, http://www.prweek.com/article/1278395/mrs -mitchell-goes-washington.

6. A full list is in the Appendix.

CHAPTER 10

1. Orion, Susan Rzepka, "Riding Right: The Friction Zone: Just What Is It, Anyway?" *Women Riders Now*, http://www.womenridersnow .com/pages/The_Friction_Zone_just_what_is_it_anyway.aspx Accessed Oct. 16, 2016.

2. Ibid.

3. That number is based on World Health Organization studies. The WHO estimate that 50 million people suffer from epilepsy and 40 million of those are in low- to middle-income countries. Of those 40 million, 30 million get no treatment. Studies show that 70 percent of epilepsy patients who get treatment see their seizures reduced to the point that they can lead normal lives.

4. Gross, Bill, "The Single Biggest Reason Why Startups Succeed," TED Talks, March 2015, www.ted.com/talks/bill_gross_the_ single_biggest_reason_why_startups_succeed.

5. "Traditions," http://www.marines.com/history-heritage/traditions, accessed Nov. 24, 2015.

CHAPTER 12

1. Here's a clip from the movie: www.youtube.com/watch?v= -dfAMTp3BAA, accessed Oct. 16, 2016.

Index

About the Author

Elise Mitchell
CEO, Mitchell
CEO, Dentsu Aegis Public Relations Network

Elise is an accomplished strategic communications professional and business leader whose entrepreneurial spirit helped build Mitchell from scratch into one of the top 10 fastest-growing firms globally, a two-time Agency of the Year winner and Inc. 500/5,000 Fastest Growing Company. The company's client portfolio includes well-known brands such as: Walmart, Procter & Gamble, Hilton Worldwide, Kraft, Del Monte, Canon, Merck, and others.

Under her leadership the company grew more than 500 percent in five years. In recognition of her accomplishments, Elise has received numerous awards including Agency Professional of the Year, Entrepreneur of the Year, and a Top 50 Power Player. At the end of 2012, Elise sold Mitchell, and today it is the leading PR agency brand in the world's fastest growing marketing communications company, Dentsu Aegis Network. In addition to her role at Mitchell, Elise is leading efforts to build a PR brand for the network.

Prior to founding Mitchell, Elise worked on both the agency and corporate sides of the business serving as the top public relations executive for Promus Hotel Corporation and holding various leadership roles at three advertising and public relations agencies.

Elise received a master's degree from the University of Memphis and a bachelor's degree from Abilene Christian University. She is a graduate of executive education training at Dartmouth College and Harvard Business School.

Elise is also a wife, mom, motorcyclist, author, and a passionate advocate for women entrepreneurs. She serves on several national boards, is a regular contributor to *Entrepreneur.com* and has a social reach of 18 million. She is a frequent keynote speaker on leadership and the secret to savoring the journey of life.

You can connect with Elise at www.elisemitchell.com or on Twitter @elisemitch.

ELISE MITCHELL

TAKE YOUR LEADERSHIP JOURNEY TO THE NEXT LEVEL

Invite Elise to Speak

Anyone who has met Elise Mitchell can attest to her energy and passion for helping others lead at their best. She brings her experiences and philosophies to life in a meaningful way with each audience she meets. You can book her for your next event at **elisemitchell.com.**

Join the Community

This book is only the beginning. Elise believes strongly in the power of community. She invites you to join the Leading Through the Turn Facebook group and become part of the conversation with other journey-minded leaders. Elise also engages with readers by sharing personal thoughts and tips on leadership via her own social media channels and email content. You can sign up for her updates and free leadership content at elisemitchell.com and follow her on social media:

 @elisemitch

 Leading Through the Turn